New Poetries V: An Anthology

MICHAEL SCHMIDT OBE FRSL is Professor of Poetry at the University of Glasgow, where he is also convenor of the Creative Writing M.Litt. Programme. He is a founder and the Editorial and Managing Director of Carcanet Press and founder and general Editor of *PN Review*. He has published several collections of poems, two novels, a number of anthologies and volumes of literary history, and two books of translations.

ELEANOR CRAWFORTH read English Literature at Cambridge before joining Carcanet Press in 2005. She has an MA in Post-1900 Literatures, Themes and Cultures from the University of Manchester. She is 'News & Notes' editor of *PN Review* and co-editor of *New Poetries IV: An Anthology* (2007). She is currently editing *Letters to an Editor*, a volume of literary correspondence from the Carcanet archive (to appear in 2012).

D0615988

Also available from Carcanet Press

New Poetries I edited by Michael Schmidt
New Poetries II edited by Michael Schmidt
New Poetries III edited by Michael Schmidt
New Poetries IV edited by Eleanor Crawforth, Stephen Procter
& Michael Schmidt

New Poetries V

An Anthology

Edited by Michael Schmidt
with Eleanor Crawforth

CARCANET

First published in Great Britain in 2011 by
Carcanet Press Limited
Alliance House
Cross Street
Manchester M2 7AQ

A CIP catalogue record for this book is available from the British Library
ISBN 978 1 84777 131 5

The publisher acknowledges financial assistance from Arts Council England

Typeset in Monotype Bembo by XL Publishing Services, Tiverton
Printed and bound in England by SRP Ltd, Exeter

Contents

Preface

Michael Schmidt

New Poetries V brings together work by twenty-two writers, many of whom will go on to publish first collections with Carcanet Press. Indeed, three of them have already done so. What will strike a reader, as it strikes the editor, is the variety of poetry represented, and the thematic range. These are poets to whose work I have responded strongly. Some of them I have been reading for years, others are more recent arrivals on my reading table; with some I have worked closely, poem by poem; with others my mission is to select. The order in which I have arranged this book is intended to emphasise the differences between the poets, to guard against any sense of a school or an emerging movement. Ford Madox Ford, the greatest editor of his age, says novelists can explore any subject, go down any avenue, but they must not propagandise, 'you must not fake any events', and later, 'your business with the world is rendering, not alteration'. The anthologist does well to follow the same advice.

On Radio 4 recently, a contemporary anthologist said he felt a compulsion to 'join arms with consensus' when choosing new poets. This puzzled me. Anthologists of new writing join arms, if at all, with new poets. Consensuses of taste or judgement or prejudice exist, of course, but are not today, thank goodness, available in the singular. A curriculum can narrow 'contemporary poetry' down to a handful of relevant and approachable writers and performers for GCSE and A-Level students. Writing programmes may homogenise the participating writers and render poetic expectation predictable. There are 'schools' associated with places and thematic or formal movements. In the book trade there are market pressures, market leaders: but the market is not a guarantor of quality in poetry or in any of the arts. The actual market nowadays is for print-hungry poets more than for poetry. Those producers can become their own consumers, buying their books for resale at readings, or to family and friends. The printed poet and the published poet are often quite different creatures.

I took a visiting Antipodean poet to a reading at Ilkley a few years ago. It marked the publication of an introductory anthology. He was bemused to hear so many 'obedient poets', he said. What forces did they obey? The modern decorums are based not on the classics, nor are they rooted in reading

Milton, Dryden or Addison. Sometimes they are rooted in not reading, a guarantee of originality of sorts.

Teachers and critics talk about 'voice', not as an instrument with which a man might, in Wordsworth's phrase, speak to men, but as an individuating medium, defined by its inflections and distinguishing mannerisms. The poem performs some kind of self, but being performative it is also ironic and the real self is withheld. Anecdote (dignified as 'narrative') displaces complex form, and the poem builds towards that audible point of (Larkin's term) 'lift-off' when the audience, if there is an audience, is conditioned to respond with the 'ooo' or 'aaa' and the intake of breath. A palpable hit. Such poems are shy of abstractions, of the 'sensuous cerebration' that Charles Tomlinson admires in the French, of the demands of traditional form and what can be done with it and experimentally against it. Ezra Pound's 'Go in fear of abstractions' has become a commandment that the obedient – obey. They go in fear, and one thing they fear is the long poem in which 'voice' is soon exhausted and other resources are required.

For magazine editors forty years ago the task of selection was easier than it is today. Whether traditional or innovative, poems were quite easily distinguished as good or bad. Now there is a third pile, sometimes the tallest of the three, where *plausible* poetry goes. Plausible writers puzzle at how poets deemed 'successful' do what they do and then attempt it themselves. Their derivations (from Paul Muldoon and John Ashbery, for example) show: what they find it hard to get is the 'through rhythm' that ensures the transitions and transformations of their sources. Robert Southey, a more exigent Poet Laureate than he is given credit for having been, and a more generous one, spoke of 'the mediocres'. He rather welcomed them because they came from different classes and they loved the art, even if they could not master it. They could be encouraged and patronised. He would be less tolerant in an age of workshops and writing programmes, when there are more writers than readers.

Editors who are not promoting a movement or a group, when they tear open an envelope or click an email attachment, hope to be surprised by the shape on the page, by syntax, by the unexpected sounds a poem makes, sometimes with old, proven instruments used in new ways. They might hope to find evidence of intelligence. And they respect creative disobedience. Where there are schools they look out for the truants; where there is a consensus with its levelling decorums, they edit against it. They are not looking for unschooled talent but for poetry as discovery in form and language. And the question of relevant subject-matter need arise only if it does arise. Nothing is prescribed.

Like its four predecessors, *New Poetries V* is an anthology of writing in the

English language, without regard to geographical divisions. Thus when I originally chose as a cover image a smiling Churchill making a Roman numeral V gesture, to signify this fifth volume, some of the poets I showed it to missed the intended irony. The poets are from Canada, England, Iran, New Zealand, the Philippines, Scotland, Singapore, South Africa and the United States. In age they range from their early twenties to their late sixties. Each has a different approach to language and form. Rather than subject them to a homogenising introductory statement, I invited all the poets to say something about their approach.

I want to express my thanks to a companion of many years without whom neither this nor any of the earlier anthologies would have come into being. That companion is *PN Review*, a magazine in which, with the enthusiasm of first love, I have been able to bring these poets new to me before a large and not uncritical readership. Several of the poets I found through the magazine, or rather, they found me. An editor can be a weary old man, opening the hundredth envelope of the week with sagging eyes. The excitement, the exclamation, which accompanies these discoveries is followed by the hope that there are growing icebergs under the glistening tips. In the case of the poets included here, there are. *PN Review* is a *vade mecum* of an organic kind, changing with the submissions it receives and changed by them, and in turn changing the editor and, I hope, some readers, to whom this, as all books, are dedicated.

Each poet has been invited to write a brief paragraph introducing the poems selected by the editors.

Tara Bergin

Most of the poems included here took me a long time to write – the idea might have been in my head for months or years. Often, they started with a line I wrote down in my notebook, such as the definition of a word, or a sentence spoken by a newsreader that I liked the sound of, or sometimes a note about the atmosphere in somebody else's poem. An example of this is my 'Himalayan Balsam' poem. I had been trying for some time to write about the wild riverbank flower which, when touched, springs back its sides and violently throws its seeds out. It was only when, as an undergraduate student, I happened to attend a lecture on Christina Rossetti's poem 'Winter: My Secret', that I found the tone I wanted. My poem is nothing like hers, but it was influenced by the ambiguity of her touch-me, touch-me-not talk. A lot of my poems seem to come about in this way; by a combination of lengthy planning and thought, followed by an unexpected resolution.

This is Yarrow

In this country house I had a dream of the city
as if the thick yarrow heads had told me,
as if the chokered dove had told me,
or the yellow elder seeds had made me ask –
and in the dream I went up to the dirty bus station
and I saw the black side of the power station
and as if the brown moth's tapping at the window
made me say it I said, do you still love me?
And when I woke and went to the window,
your tender voice told me: this is yarrow,
this is elder, this is the collared dove.

Portrait of the Artist's Wife as a Younger Woman

I go to my husband's studio
and I stand looking at her face,
hearing only:
tick-tock, tick-tock.

I stand and I think:
I must measure seven ounces at three.
I must level the scoops with a clean dry knife.
(he wanted a wife he wanted a wife) –
I must pick up the baby with its shaking fist,
and go: Shh, shh, little one,
while I sprinkle the milk
like perfume on my wrist,
it's so hot, little one, it's so sour, little thing.

I look at her there.
See where the soft knife's been
at her collarbone and her mouth
which is pink –
like the bark of trees in America,
in the south.

And she doesn't say:
I am free legally to take;
she doesn't say: Shh, shh.
Only I speak.
Only I say: Shh, shh.
Only I say: it's so hot, little one,
it's so sour, little thing.

Rapeseed

He thought my clothes were my skin.
He thought these soft things,
this lace and these buttons,
were things I belonged in,
but I do not belong in them.
I told him but he didn't see.

Look, he went on stroking my gloves
and my things,
thinking, what fine skin – Oh
Mister My, My –
I did take thee and thou me.
And after the ceremony?
Quiet, quiet.

We drove past rapeseed.
Fields of it through the window
on the full hot air – oh sweet,
oh stale, oh clinging to the air –
oh shame, oh full, oh cruel.

How we feared its fierceness!
How we worried it would overlook us!
We feared too much,
thinking the world
is reached only in violence.

You Could Show a Horse

An experiment in collage

You could show a horse, *you might see some riderless horse*, galloping among the *rushing among the enemy* with its mane in the wind *with his mane flying in the wind* causing heavy casualties *and doing no little mischief with his heels.* Or you could show a man, mutilated, *some maimed warrior may be seen* lying on the ground *fallen to the earth* shielding himself in some way *covering himself with his shield* with his enemy bent over him and trying to *while the enemy bending over him tries to deal him a deathstroke* – or show a lot of people fallen on to a dead horse *A number of men fallen in a heap over a dead horse* – and you could show the men *you would see some of the victors*, leaving the fight, *abandoning the conflict* emerging from the *and issuing from the crowd* using both hands *rubbing their eyes and cheeks with both hands*, to clean their faces, *to clean them of the dirt made by their watering eyes* now coated *smarting from the dust and smoke* in tears which have poured from their dust-filled eyes.

Questions

1.   Did you ever play the piano again after your mother died and if so, what did you play?

2.   Could you sing and did you ever sing later on in life when you were married and living away from Moscow?

3.   If you can remember (and please try) what songs exactly did you sing?

4.   What did you think when you took your pen in your hand and wrote that letter to Stalin?

5.   Did you feel a kind of heat of the mind and also a chill somewhere in your stomach?

6.   Did your hand shake?

7.   Is time mostly to do with feeling and thought?

8.   Is time a trap, in your opinion?

9.   Am I completely responsible for what I do with time, or not at all, or partly?

10. How powerful – would you say – is a poem not to do with war?

11. Did you like the violin?

12. Were you an insomniac?

13. Compared, I mean, to one about war?

The Undertaker's Tale of the Notebook Measuring 1 x 2 cm

For forty years I have had in my possession:
A notebook, morocco-bound and blue in colour
which was so small it could be covered over by a thumb.
I found it at the bottom of her
apron pocket;

And for forty years I have had in my throat
the rotten apple of Mordovia
which for forty years
I could not swallow;

And I have held in my possession
the year Nineteen-Forty-
One:
a year too small for her
to write in.

Military School

The analysis of battle begins here at our desks.
The voice of violence enters our mouths
and our skin, and under my own nails
I hear it seduce me. I argue with nothing it says.
The voice is a swan of the estuary.
It laments, it recites:
Sixteen Dead Men; The Rose Tree,
out of pages yellowed from 1953 –
it bangs oh it bangs
a bodhran.
I agree.
I denounce my motherland,
propose fidelity to my fatherland.
It begins here,
the voice of beauty begins here,
lovely out of the desk.
We mark our youth on the
photocopied maps with black crosses,
obediently we mark our youth.

Red Flag

Once one of them showed me how to:
You turn this (the right) hand to grasp the stock.
You turn this (the left) hand to grasp the barrel.
He touched my knee,
and I hid my surprise –
but now he's changed his tune.

36, 37, 38.9

I've a fever little sparrow, I am sick.
Their flag is flying red,
I can hear it from my window,
I hear it tattered like a torn red rag.
Go and get it little bird,
go and tell them danger! danger!

I will wear it as my Sunday Dress.
I'll wear it walking on the moor
where they practice with their guns.

38.9, 37, 36

How ashamed they'll be
to hurt a young and pretty
girl like me.

Swiss Station Room

Dear Anne, what a show –
my tongue was going
like the red second hand
on that clock, on that clock
at the station, did you see it?
When he watched me –
Did you see how my cheeks
were flushed – how my cheeks were hot?
Did you see how my hands on my lap
pulled and twisted at my dress –
Could he see? How shy?
I spoke vainly: it was false.

Liebe Anne, you spoke so much better,
like a man, like a bull –

Ay ay ay –
it's becoming
it's becoming habitual
and I…

How vain the sea is also, though,
have you noticed?
Gazing forever in the glass,
always avoiding, avoiding us both.

Glinka

Look at little Mikhail Ivanovich:

five flights up in his grandmother's room,
wrapped in furs, and perched like a pianist
on her padded, crocheted, dressing-table stool –

Porter! Grandmother calls.
Keep the thermostat at twenty-five degrees –

Mikhail eats sweets,
wrapped and stuffy in his furs.
On Sunday he hears the sound of the street:
a choir, five flights down.

Meeka, Meeka,
come away from the window.

Grandmother wrings her hands.
The village church rings her bell.
Young Mikhail knows all is well.

Himalayan Balsam for a Soldier

They don't see me but I walk
into Fitzgeralds with them the half-wounded,
I sit in there at the high table with my pint,
half-wounded, thinking, I will drag my
wounds in here.
I drag myself in and up to the high stool
among the guys with one arm and they
don't see me.
Here is your talisman I say, I whisper
hold it in your good hand and sing one
of your songs for me.
How does it go? Oh how does it go again?
There is blood on my hand, la la,
there is blood on my hand, la, la.
Your talisman, I say, a foul flower.
Hold it in your hand and how full your good
hand will be with the
exploding.

If Painting Isn't Over

If painting isn't over
I will say this:
Who have I offended?

1. I have figures that are not figures;
2. I have gone for an undoing of the image.

If painting isn't over
I will admit this:
You have offended your whole life.
You have divided your days.
You have taken your hands
and put them in the drawer.

Oli Hazzard

Form is helpful for me as a way of orientating myself amongst the bric-a-brac (to gobble Frost's nibble at Stevens) of words and sensation, providing a narrative and/or organisational template to adhere to, work against, or ignore. Many of these poems started life as mistakes – misheard or misunderstood words, sounds or images taken for others, gutted anecdotes, punchlines cut adrift from their jokes – so it often seems right to carry on from this first impetus. It's a little cruel, maybe, to set an already dyspraxic thing hobbling across an old obstacle course, but after all the stress and amputations, by the end it can be gratifyingly unrecognisable. This estrapade reaches its logical extreme in 'The Inability to Recall the Precise Word for Something', which is a 'found' poem (a bad case of messiah-desire); I tried to be as absent-minded about my selections as possible, but, no matter how significant the disjunction between lines, narrative and identification always seemed to occur. So now I like to read this poem as part of a dialogue between two poems, the one included here, made up of definitions, and the one elsewhere, made of their words.

Moving In

You take me down to the crease in the hills
Where the farm's boundaries are smothered
By brambles and the dry stream-bed lies
Like a pelt – we follow it quietly, shoeless,
Listening to the waves at Calpe knead into
The beach, and reaching out my hand to
Touch your hair we are suddenly
Aware of the sensation that we are being
Overheard: yet all there is on this side
Of the valley is the fuzz of telephone
Wires overhead and darkness slowly
Encroaching behind the skin-pink clouds –
The orange trees, after all, seem to clutch themselves
Above the safflowers and alfalfas that
Spring from the ground like cocked eyebrows –
So, stepping onwards – stalking, by now –
Convinced that night is simply the folding over
Of fingers, leaned into a steeple – we hunt
For some burrow, some hood of earth
Where the sound of the sea is as unbroken
As it is within a coiled shell and build
A fire whose voice, like chicks-being-
Incessantly-hatched, will make our
Own seem all the more improbable. But
Now, as I sit alone, crumbling dry leaves
In my palm, it seems all I can dream of is
The onset of sleep. Really, I hardly notice
The rising heat of the circling brush fire that
Flays the whole sky of its stars.

True Romance

1

The window I saw myself in was a room.
The sun unpacked the buildings. On the deep table
An antique map, bleached of its colours, lay twitching in
The breeze, a drowsy mantis. I drifted beneath a honeycomb of balloons;
Mistook swans for dollops of cream; saw ghosts in
The white of Chinese-burned skin. Those people
Inside looked out at me strangely. They couldn't
Believe it when I reached out to touch them. I said, We all believe
In the value of pretending one thing is another, don't we?
We were all a little frightened. But I could not do what
I threatened. Something else was needed to secure it in place.
Said another way, maybe it could have happened.

2

Said another way, maybe it could have happened,
I threatened. Something else was needed to secure it in place.
We were all a little frightened. But I could not – what?
In the value of pretending one thing is another. Don't we
Believe it? When I reached out to touch them, I said: *we all believe.*
Inside looked out at me strangely. They couldn't.
The white of Chinese-burned skin, those people –
Mistook swans for dollops of cream, saw ghosts in
The breeze. A drowsy mantis, I drifted. Beneath a honeycomb of balloons,
An antique map, bleached of its colours, lay twitching.
The sun unpacked the buildings on the deep table.
The window I saw myself in was a room.

Prelude To Growth

Tomorrow is watching today through the one-way mirror.
Something is taken from each, exchanged for something else, more
or less valuable.

Your too-thick glasses, the ones that
are totally off-trend, render the suddenly swarming pavilions
a tearful furnace.

No one is more or less orange. Microbes of sand grow
on my eyes. The collision between cement-mixer and ice-cream van
provokes less identity

in the etiolated gallantry of longhand. Make milk my measure
of white. Or today a smaller fraction of my life.
To oil that lends water a gradient.

And yet the gorgeous weather continues to move along
the walls,
plucks the Dijon telephone, approves its endurance.

Now your hand hovers
over each object: it self-inflates to meet the bruit gift.
As these beaches

remain leaning into their own portrait,
in that fuller night, our skin powdery, we see the whole event
unfolding very slowly,

the wind somersaulting down our throats.

The Inability To Recall The Precise Word For Something

All things are words of some strange tongue
Jorge Luis Borges

The first person you see after leaving your house
One who always wants to know what's going on
To make money by any means possible
A surgical sponge accidentally left inside a patient's body
Given to incessant or idiotic laughter
An incestuous desire for one's sister
The act of mentally undressing someone
One who speaks or offers opinions on matters beyond their knowledge
A secret meeting of people who are hatching a plot
The act of beating or whipping school children
The categorisation of something that is useless or trivial
Belching with the taste of undigested meat
One who is addicted to abusive speech
The use of foul or abusive language to relieve stress or ease pain
The condition of one who is only amorous when the lights are out
To blind by putting a hot copper basin near someone's eyes
The act of opening a bottle with a sabre
The habit of dropping in at mealtimes
The act of killing every twentieth person
One who eats frogs
The low rumbling of distant thunder
Someone who hates practicing the piano
The practice of writing on one side of the paper
A horse's attempt to remove its rider
The collective hisses of a disapproving audience
The sensation that someone is mentally undressing you
The act of self-castration
Being likely to make a mistake
One who fakes a smile, as on television
Counting using one's fingers
The act or attitude of lying down
The smell of rain on dry ground
The space between two windows

Source: http://users.tinyonline.co.uk/gswithenbank/unuwords.htm

Apologia

His stillness knows exactly what it wants. Flemish, it climbs
down the rungs of its laughter, til strasse-light chokes
in the key of its throat, or a reticulated fog catches
in the youngish trees; or, through the milk-bottle glaucoma
of a villainous monocle, it scouts out the gallery of a plot-hatchery
with a test-tube full of bewitching molecules. Thwarted! In the long hiss of
its head,
thawing silence slakes the fossilising song *Their Life is Hidden with God.*

Some song! Like a soft cymbal it shirrs in the recollection.
The city's plushness crab-hands along the neck
of its buildings. Who trusts such plushness, huh? (Does *who* fuck?)
It neither declares intentions nor inters declensions.
Playing it backwards reveals a song being force-fed itself (the *tack-tock-tuck-tick*
of drool from its mouth). Scuppered, he lounges against the scene-stripping
window: tries to name, then count, then watch, the flux of birds palpitating

in the sprained lens of a lake, a jigsaw shaken out of its box,
indicating, in a shaky hand, that the shape's clear, the picture less so.
Cheap tricks earn cheap treats, *brother,* he mutters, before, like the sudden
urge to
feign sleep, an obscure and untrustworthy impulse selects
the sensation, then turns it over to itself: do what you have to, (Baltimore,
simpatico)
but make it quick. But his stillness could outrun itself. Decades without
water!
Then: We don't seem to have moved. *Then:* Every move an altar.

As Necessity Requires

An emptiness returns to surround the books, lamps, apple-cores
and photographs, until the room is a cupboard full of cans
with their labels removed. The distended, much thumbed reflection
is plain and repetitious, as the texture of the silence between the effort

and the inability becomes a noise rubbed so hard, and so long,
it seems to hallucinate a source upon its surface. In this slow frieze
of inertia, such mistakes are lent a barely credible uniformity,
yet fall back through the embellished openings of embarrassment
to place each one at its starting point, a fresh fixity in its gaze,
as though the distance had rolled itself up into a welcome mat
that could be covered in a single stride. So this is your home:
tell me how much you recognise. In the phlox of the brain, home means a
                                                        diorama
in which the setting and the species are the same. But earliest details
are porous as the most tender plot, the peripheries bordered with
breathed-upon glass, an opportune spray of tendrils, the humid fuzz
tuned in by the elastic mollusc of an eyeball. Something in
the corner sets a clear blister in the blurring air; softens, then hardens, into
the stillness required, an outstretched hand trying to steady itself.

The required stillness descended, having run naked into the plexiglass.
The reverberations thrummed along the windows of the other exhibits;
those with tongues to the glass picked up the low note
of slapstick misery, turned either in pity or terror to capture
the event's rotations, then reported in a manner that identified, then secured,
the syntax of their feeling; alcoves and swiftly branching passages tuned
the pulse of the air-conditioning to an arhythmical drone. And yet recesses
continue to appear in the shucked resemblances of earlier hours, their
own kind of numb learning, continuously filled with fragrant
and explosive fluids, as sunlight is pulled down into a building. These
become thoughts that don't know they're thoughts. Later, bridges
that hunt their own breaking. When it comes, it is like seeing
a memory for the first time. The easy guilt of noticing that
nothing else rises to the brim of this jar – this puffs it out a little further,
elevates it in degrees of thousands of feet, until its size is such
that to look down from it would be to fall, which would be a sort of answer,
perhaps, but to a completely different, less necessary question; of the tension
in hollowed air. Or, how large we need ourselves to become.

Sonnet

The vast pumpkin-coach sprays ochre dust
On the finely-etched grain: *how many* brassy-gleaming
Coins flung to clatter amongst the crowds' gurgling
Clishmaclaver, *how many* phosphorescent
Torques hung...? No will's as strong
As a cloud in which a voice mumbles, engulfing
Its audience with an adolescent strum, or
Better yet (hoarsely now) the pyx-bound diarchy
Propped upon a burnished palm! Yet over the bristling
Ice-chafed land the foghorns disperse, eventually running out
Of twine; the cliffs lean and shift like pale passengers
Squashed against the pane; the sea shirrs
Against itself, hissing, unfurled, of its irreversible wane...
Standing here, I count myself, and count myself again.

A Walking Bird

When we wade out together
through the scrolls of brackish water, dispersing
the long rainbow-nets, the frail networks
        of foam and grease, the brief, glyptic
                reflections of branches and twigs
        spidering the surface –
'we'll need something more than this...'

So we return to the hearth
joking that death is a matter of proof, if
I'm willing to follow my argument
        through: the wind gargles itself in
                the chimney, the thunder outside
        rolls its stone across the cave-
mouth, and they retain a youth

of sorts, though only to younger
ears than yours: 'Who endures such oneiric
phenomena when there's a world outside
      to be civilised?' you say, scrunch-
          ing up papers for kindling –
    as daffodils spring from
logs, shadows roam the ceiling.

With Hindsight

The way to the stomach is through the heart.
If he's been eating with his eyes, ask him exactly how much
He's been beholding. If his words are drowned out
By his actions, tell him not to protest so much.

A little yearning is a dangerous thing; he clearly hasn't been
Eating his apple-a-day. If only the incision were skin-deep.
No wonder he's blind. But even a worm will turn –
Softly, softly – from a piece of string to a length of old rope.

But give him enough and he'll hang.
If God had meant us to fall, he'd have given us wings –
But then there'd be no work for drinkers.
So, those who cannot preach, practice.
Truth is wasted on the tongue.

Old-Fashioned Uncouth Measurer

Il y a une horloge qui ne sonne pas
Arthur Rimbaud

Something clear melts where I come by – as though
I were a thing caught in the day's throat.
Through the emptier stretches rosy fluids grow dark and wet
the incessant waking, switching on light
and pointless light: *jog thou on*, we repeated, under
breath, towards an authentic contraption levered
high in the entrance-hall –
make a habit of the stake we've all made. Still,
with hunger like a mirror persuading
we caught on to our own moving
and sought out a moisture to restore it. The span between silences
buckled in our averted nerves.
Now the breeze lifts the networks of leaves from the staircase
like your daughter's resemblances of fish.
They are, apparently, more true,
you tell me:
as in the vault of those fingers
my own was kept cold, less false.

from Home Poems

They that swell into a hovering blimp of summer, that cross-breed with other
people's faces, that are better prepared for bad news by a film, that though
they normally hate Tom Hanks, that go to all the speciality stores and talk
with the assistants, that flee the knowledge that all cities are like, that stand in
Trafalgar Square with a sack of fresh zebra meat, that are like a walking preg-
nancy test, that no-one dare take, that are hus and a d w e, that a e h sband
and if, that re hu b n an w fe, that squabble over the bill, that are both bill
and embarrassed waiter, that have arranged for a set of keys to be cut, that
climb sideways through the woods, that, that have, that have slowed the
cabling of fish to the surface, that sign themselves as T. Hanks and look weary,
that is not quite finished with you yet young, that are atrophied insistence,

that caulk the plump nest of the brain's intention, that are a quiet advocate of crunk, that pixellate their own sound as it comes when the lights go off and on very quickly cannot remember the name they should not have said.

They that leave love-bites upon my neck, that abhor the gathering of flies in clusters, that when the ground gave way did not, that at the culling of vertigo can laughter, that is what is meant by, that with birds & physicians ripen dunes in air before noon sink postcards into the thought of snowstorms.

They that conduct tailbacks in my Russian dreams, that thatch gums with lovelorn cattle-prods, that assume an anchor in a bed of sun, that stop short of hay, that plummet like tulips into the unbroken river, that are stepping too quickly into the middle of a queue, that is not moving fast enough for the yellow and green cars, that are either too miserable to face-paint today, that have to drink the colour bottle-green, that cannot play this afternoon because she stepped on a razor, that looks at the mirror as a photograph, that collate all species of pet reluctance, that teach advanced ice-cream van at the graduate school this semester are all sporting aviator jackets the colour of water.

They that let the dogs run out in the road, that have unstitched the ice-cubes, that my knowing thickened into a grainy paste, that became an embassy to this bravado of blessings, that the weather cannot absorb, that decided that it, that distil deer from insurance company calendars, that reap the palest archaism from a thirty-three-year-old passport holder who, that with others did commit, that I may honour regularly clink sun-rays in thespian midnight.

James Womack

Looking at these ten poems, I am struck by the amount of boasting and lying that goes on throughout them. Also, only three of them (including, disgracefully, 'Vomit') have their roots in my own personal experience, although seven of them are written in the first person singular and invite the reader to imagine a narrative figure who is in some ways close to the poet himself. Even the most seemingly heartfelt poems tend to come from my reading rather than my life. Some acknowledgements: 'Complaint' is a loose translation from Propertius; 'The Dogs of a House in Mourning and the Naked Girl' is based on an essay by the film director Nagisa Oshima, found in *Cinema, Censorship and the State* (The MIT Press, 1993); 'Don't Look Back, Lonesome Boy' is a translation of a poem by the Cuban writer Luis Rogelio Nogueras. 'La chute de la maison Usher' was written after seeing Jean Epstein's 1928 film of the same name, one of the first movies Luis Buñuel worked on as an assistant director. Some details in 'Tourism' come from oral testimony gathered and reported by Marfua Tokhtakhodzhaeva in her book *The Re-Islamisation of Society and the Position of Women in Post-Soviet Uzbekistan*, the manuscript of which I corrected in some small town, one indifferent summer. SPOILER ALERT. 'Balance' was written in September 2001, when everything seemed to be up in the air. SPOILERS END.

Complaint

Death is not the end; some doors are never fully closed,
and hollow ghosts escape their coffins and ovens.
She had been – she is – buried in rowdy Madrid,
but last night, as I held myself in a breaking sleep,
Carlota came to me and leant over my uneasy bed.
She was like her photographs, the same steady eyes;
her right ankle still had its tattoo. But her skin was broken,
and her clothes were rags covered with dirt and clay.
She was there, she could speak, I knew it was her,
though the thumb-bones creaked in her fragile hands.
'How can you sleep,' she said, 'how can you sleep?
I knew this would happen, that you'd forget it all:
the window-sill where my arms wore two smooth dents,
the code to my staircase, the heavy metal doors.
We broke into a fire-watchers' tower and saw the city –
do you remember? – saw the city and made promises.
Were those light promises, are you allowed to forget?
Where were you when I died? Did you do anything?
If you had cried out for me to come back, I could have
at least for one day, I could have held myself alive,
but nobody, not you, not Julius, Arima, nobody…
None of you even knows where I am buried.
Would it cost you too much to find out, find me?
Is there anybody who talks about me with love,
who remembers me as I was, not just as someone
who died, who died young, who died too young?
You deserve to have me haunt you, keep you awake,
hurt you… but what's the use? You'll write your poems
which turn me into some amalgam of memory
and adolescent hard-on: I'm safe for you to use now.
Even these hands that grasp you, even these hands,
they'll just be one more image among the others.
At least I have been faithful, I haven't forgotten,
I remember you well and keep my mouth shut.
You can't negotiate with me: my arguments are fixed,
and I will keep my counsel.'
                              She touched my shoulder
and I reached up to her, those remembered arms

and her torso cold and so thin. But she twisted away,
propped herself on her elbows and looked into my face.
'Find me. Do what you can for me, for my body.
Stop writing about me. I am not, I am not material
for you to appropriate and employ. Clean my grave,
lay some flowers there, give me an epitaph:
not one of your self-indulgent look-at-mes,
but something simple and worthy, for visitors
to read and understand. Of course, keep writing
but leave me out of it. And find other women
while you live: when you are dead you will be mine
alone, and we together shall be dust and ashes.'
She stopped talking, and lay down beside me,
but when I opened my eyes, my arms were empty.

after the Latin of Propertius

The Dogs of a House in Mourning and the Naked Girl

The nameless village is burned out
alongside a red clay road dried white.
This is no temporary silence –
April is hot, and the grass stinks.

I came here through a rabbit-hole
in the sagged wire fence.
Two dogs ran from a dead house.
I held my camera between us, snapping.

As a child I had a nightmare of wolves
but now I thought of the proverb
Thin as a dog in the house of mourning.
One grey dog, one spotted like a tiger.

Beyond their teeth and noise
was the shadow of something not a dog.
Children in the doorway of a broken building:
a five-year-old girl, a boy, an older girl.

Silhouettes in rags, almost naked;
and in the house two more girls moving faintly.
.I couldn't make out their poses or expressions,
I kept taking photographs.

The barking dogs had disappeared.
I went down to the road
and stopped people to ask about it all:
some soldiers, a bus driver, a couple of farmers.

Tourism

As the soldiers grow older, they turn native
And grow their beards, against all posted orders.
Duty troops roll in for the tour: they are all naïve,
So keen to pick up the language. Yesterday's doctors

Are trading in the city as shoe-shine boys,
Yesterday's bankers work in second-hand shops –
They deal in tyres and scrap iron and flotsam and toys
Made from flotsam and tyres and iron scrap.

Inquisitive cults grow up around petrol
Bottles and rags. Religion is being reborn.
The factories work at half their potential.
Psst! Want to know something? Well, not everyone

*Has – or wants – a historical homeland they'd love
To return to.* The restaurants are forever
Closed for health reasons; the mosques are moved
With the quince trees still inside and the pillars

Intact. *Do you want to pay me?* A cold war
Leaves ruins, like any other war. Life moves,
Only just. Look, dressed in national costume, here
Come the women, strapped to their bundles of gifts.

'Don't Look Back, Lonesome Boy'

Slowly and patiently we have forgotten it all.
When we made the nails tremble in the headboard
And you rose up with a whisper, the gentle surf moaning.
Underneath the voices, a guitar sounded on the radio.
We believed (at least I believed) in the strength of our arms,
In the precise detail, proof against anything, of our faltering liquid memories,
In the absolute power of those poems I wrote
When I slid barefoot from bed – I scribbled them blindly,
While you were sleeping,
On any old paper, in a book.
There are so many beautiful, serious, urgent words that will stay forgotten.
I thought the only worthwhile writing was direct and shameless.

To love you,
While things were like this, while they stayed like this as you slept, naked,
And I had a scrap of paper, or the wall,
Or some blank corner of the planet;
We thought then that the guitar, the damn guitar, would keep on playing.

Tonight I realised how little life costs, and you and I did not know this.
Tonight a shadow, any shadow
Is enough to blow out that strong, eternal, indestructible flame,
Any south wind will be enough to blot out my voice.
Memory is water which runs dry
And we cannot (at least, I cannot)
Remember for example that other night
Which we thought inhabited only by you and me and our words.
(Was it raining? What did we do? What did we say?)
A man who turns to face the past is blind
Because he forgets things twice;
How touching, to try to look with love on the ashes of a love;
As touching as those clowns who contort their bodies by night,
In the middle of the deserted marquee,
And throw their harsh voices into the empty tiers.

after the Spanish of Luis Rogelio Nogueras

Experiment

Lived life backwards for a week or so – Ovaltine for breakfast, a long hot
bath, bacon and eggs and a pint of coffee at about midnight.

Ten days in, unmoving, nocturnal, costive, bawling for my mother,
wearing school uniform again.

Vomit

Never as sick as after: homemade thick
chicken liver paté,
½ a bottle of *Stalinswein* (which we bought as a joke,
but no, not funny, not funny…)

The effort I'd been to, the livers so light –
snipping out over the sink
the involved white root –
and the water draining pink.

Then, the lineaments of what I had done, there
on the bedroom floor,
and the room heaved and heavy.
O yes, this was God's plenty.

But as the morning reeled by
all I could remember was the uncooked offal:
these little organs, light as some baby,
and I felt more awful.

Balance

It didn't want to let the morning
Come, as if the globe were rocking back,
Back and forwards, twisting gently like
A fair-day weathervane, and turning
Towards the sun, turning us away.
Calm but firm, the world like a mother
Did not allow it to be either
One thing or the other, night or day.
The sky was gritty with darkness, with
The light and the dark mixed, for the air
Was full of masonry-dust, plaster,
Powder, snowflakes, soot. I thought that if
I tore the page off the calendar
The next page would have the same number.
It didn't want to let morning come.
Fine by us. But the mechanism
Slips suddenly out of gear – we are
Jerked forward, lose balance once more.
This is the last station in autumn –
The sun is up, the scales have fallen.

La chute de la maison Usher

i.m. Jean Epstein (1897–1953), and all the rest

The camera running down a corridor full of leaves.

The bridal veil falls like river-weed.

Her neck is a long white smear of paint.

A life lit only by candles.

A sudden white square as the reel ends.

Veronica Lake, Zasu Pitts, Marguerite Gance...
all gone out of the world of light:
Whisper it softly: they are all dead.
Not just the stars, but the shadows in the dark
who went to gaze on them.

The camera running down.

A corridor full of leaves.

And all the world outside – a swamp;
a little dog that runs from him.

Little Red Poem

If they ask for me tell them I have gone away
to lead my people and be led by them;
to take the thorny path that leads to the light
to struggle, suffer and finally prevail.

Tell them the only home a man can hope for
if he wish to prove his life worthwhile
is the struggle to create a home for all mankind,
not the lone sad fight from one day to the next.

Tell them that if they want me they shall find
my thoughts in others' books, in others' words,
that I am nothing but an honest vessel,
a witness to the truth and not the truth itself.

But do not tell them I am in the attic
behind the false partition, biting my arm in fear,
my gun by my side; that, although reluctant,
I could, at a pinch, employ it for the cause.

freely adapted from the Slovenian

Now, / A / Poem / That is called / 'Of Insomnia'

All tricks fail. I have tried lying
on my back, my side, on my belly, diagonal;
I have tried less duvet, many
blankets, scooched to the coolest parts of this nocturnal
world, overwarmed them with my flesh.
I am jealous of my sleeping wife and my two cats
dormant nose to anus like a
perverse ginger yin-yang. I have counted quadrupeds,
bipeds, unicycles, counted
the first hundred terms of the Fibonacci series,
counted the clock marking an hour,
and am counting inevitably my ex-girlfriends,
dividing them into two camps:
Inaccessible (Distant), Inaccessible (Dead);
and more sex than I could stand for
nowadays has been recalled, salvaged and catalogued.
I have hoped for inspiration;
have only had memory, physical discomfort.
I am empty. The bedroom is
a black box. I am glad not to remember it all,
to have to remember it all,
save image after image after afterimage
on what must be the limited
discspace of my brain. I remember other bedrooms
and car headlights on the ceiling.
My wakefulness has sifted that picture from the night.

Lucy Tunstall

My poems are concerned with moments of family history, and difficulties of personal communication which seem (but perhaps are not) a particularly English affliction: a great uncle really did drive a traction engine from Windsor to Isleworth, but no one can can remember why; during the Blitz, my father and uncles really were sent away from London to a school under the flight path where returning enemy planes occasionally unloaded unused ammunition before crossing the Channel. These are small episodes or simple narratives which I find in some way telling, or faintly ridiculous, or both.

Looking over this selection I notice that my work features charismatic female figures, who may be benign or malign, and my speaker is often a rather inward child. I am not sure what to make of this.

My themes and subjects are sometimes dramatic and I am interested in the ways in which poetry that would claim to speak from the heart, must also acknowledge its theatrical components and motivations.

The Vulgar Muse

You have come out of the bitter lake.
You have come sliding towards me with set jaw.
You have rolled in with the fog and the drear
and pressed me to your flaccid breast.
Sparks fly from your dress.
Your hair is like the warrior's helmet.
Your skin is white as the corpse, and your hair black.
You have stopped my nostrils with your scent
and my throat with your powder.
You have dressed me in your heavy red with tissues in the pocket.
You have taken from me the flagon and the bread
and you have fed me ashes and salt.
You have taken from me my soft skin, my hope
and all my treasures, my bible and the carpet from my feet,
and nothing, nothing have you given me.

Estate

Cousin Gillian lives in a caravan by the shores of a lake in Canada, and in that caravan,
so they say, she keeps Grandmother Elizabeth's long-case clock.

Some people do not think this is an appropriate arrangement.
They think it is heartless of her to keep such a fine piece
(school of Tompion) in such a dread abode.
Heartless and unthinking. How could she?
But I think it is a fine thing
which I would like to behold.

Is there a special orifice or protuberance of some kind
in the roof of the caravan through which or into which the clock extends?
Does it lean jauntily within, and does this have any adverse effect on the
mechanism?
Do the bears and moose rouse to its bong! bong! bong!?
How could such a wonder be, in any way, wrong?

It may be scooped out like a canoe
circling the lake at dawn and dusk; there would be room
for a packed lunch and the catch.
It might be a barricade, staunch
against the creatures of the night; it might be
out in all weathers; may serve as makeshift bench or table.
It might be firewood, a folly, or a totem pole;
it's possible, we just don't know.

Oh Gillian, cousin of my right hand! Cousin I have never met!
Let me, if some will not, bestow with happy heart
this ancient clock, to do with just as you see fit,
in praise of *self*-possession and the pioneering spirit.

Traction

My mother's grandmother wore black for years and years,
lived among laurel and yew in a lodge at the big house,
where Charlie, her unmarried brother, slept under the eaves
on a sort of ledge. No one knows why it was Charlie
took off, slow as slow, with nothing for the journey
but an onion and a piece of sharp cheese, to pilot his
traction engine, by a seam of moonlight on the river,
as far east as Isleworth, by way of Maidenhead and Old Windsor.

During the Blitz

Elizabeth stayed on in Greenwich, where her husband was employed in
counter-espionage broadcasting for the BBC, and, simultaneously, a cere-
bral and stimulating relationship with his secretary, Kathleen.

Elizabeth saw that the biscuit barrel was polished, that no scraps were wasted, and barely flinched when a particularly heavy raid blew in the windows of the front elevation; shards of glass impaled themselves in the staircase and the panelling.

The children, now to be known only as major and minor, were removed to a progressive school in Kent where the playing fields, conveniently bordered on one side by a deep trench, lay directly beneath the flight path of the incoming Luftwaffe.

In the dark, after lights-out, their father's words swam on through the ether, *Liebling, mein liebling, my pigeon, my dove.*

Aunt Jane and the Scholar

In 1956, or thereabouts,
Aunt Jane fell in love with a beautiful
scholar from the subcontinent.

Her house is tall and thin like a doll's house.
Pictures are filling in the walls,
but where the paint shows through in a chink
it is the authentic dull pink of oxblood and lime.

We take tea in the garden which is like a well
with its high walls, and deep shade and the underwater
grey-green of the thyme lawn; and sitting still like a still
ancient cloistered thing at the bottom of a well

she remembers (she must remember) a long trip
to the only part of Canada where it never snows,
weeks and weeks of sky and sea and sickness like snow-sickness.

Ever after a drawing-in, this square
of London sky, and the cypress leaning over.

One Day a Herd of Wild Horses Came into the Garden and Looked at My Mother

Well, this is extraordinary, she is saying, *this is quite extraordinary.*

The horses stand on the grass and look at my mother.
My mother stands on the path and looks at the horses.
The horses nudge and shift; their manes tangle; their hooves are caked in mud.

Not until the mare has turned her head, like a sail in the wind, away from
      the house and out toward the hills, and led each straggling foal away,
                          will my mother go
back into the house; close the door; pick up a book, a coffee, a cigarette.

Thin

In an eyrie by the Thames, my mother is preparing for the summit.
What used to be a first floor flat has grown higher and higher.
Even at base camp the air is thin. She is very high up.
She watches us all in her magnifying mirror, or doesn't bother.
Tea, cigarette, coffee, aspirin, cigarette, cigarette, wine, cigarette.
Cigarette, cigarette, cigarette, as the night draws in.
The days wax and wane. Soon it may be necessary to boil snow.
She is preparing her physical body for an extraordinary feat.
She is trying on her dresses. She is Wallis Simpson-thin.
Today, tomorrow or the next day, is the day she must be gone.

Remembering the Children of First Marriages

Oh remember the children of first marriages
For they are silent and awkward in their comings and their goings;
For the seal of the misbegotten is upon them;
For they walk in apology and dis-ease;
For their star is sunk;
For their fathers' brows are knitted against them;
For they bristle and snarl.
All you light-limbed amblers in the sun,
Remember the grovellers in the dark,
The scene-shifters, the biders, the loners.

Idyll

Two frogs and a toad,
each scarcely bigger
than a money spider,
have come into the house
in the furl of a leaf,
in the cluster of small
green hearts which spills in
under the back door,
making, of the leaking
roof and the creeping
damp, a garden.

Not Playing the Dane

He liked – or said he liked – best of all
a brief cameo in the final act,
a decent armchair in the dressing room,
not too much to learn, nothing *experimental*
no doubling up, no hanging on for curtain call.

Pantomime

I was one of those children who had to be coaxed.
The dancing-girl zeroed in, inviting, all teeth and eyes.
Yes, yes, bobbed the father attached to her head.
No, no, no, no said my fingers clutching the underside
of the red velvet seat where the nap was still good,
take the others; take the other children instead.
As they all clambered eagerly on to the stage I relaxed
my grip, put my theatrical career on ice.

1976

We were not to mention the gold teeth
of Pedro, Nicaraguan prince and companion
of my godfather, Barry J. Gordon. All through lunch
the sunlight screeched off Pedro's canines
igniting the cutlery, the pine cladding,
the tomato-red kitchen cabinets.

⋆

While my godfather swore blind the Staffordshire
pottery spaniel – seventeenth-century, royalist, red-haired –
belonged to him, *I want that fucking dog,*
my mother – regal, carolean – gave no ground,
Darling, you are *dreadful.* My father slunk about,
not up to the game, rightly punished.

⋆

By a curious and intricate choreography
my father made his way to my bedroom,
mapped out a constellation in phosphorescent stars,
retreated, reversing all the steps, leaning close in
to the dado, avoiding the creaky stair, was far away
when the lights went down, the applause began.

Alex Wylie

I am impelled by history and by the multifarious possibilities of what's often called love poetry. When I review what I have written over the past few years, I realise that what motivates my thought and feeling is a sense that all value derives from relationships of some sort, be they political, intellectual, sexual, to do with friendship, or between individuals and history. My poems explore the tension between traditional forms and the individual voice, and between the cosmopolitan and the local. I am interested in the political place of poetry, though I am still uncertain what that place may be.

The poems selected here were written between 2004 and 2011. 'Of Scaurus, a Rich Man and Covetous' is a version of a fifteenth-century Latin satire by Tito Strozzi. The eponymous subject of 'Epitaph on Elizabeth Barton, the Nun of Kent' was an English Joan of Arc; at the age of seventeen she began to speak in rhyming prophecies, possibly as the result of what we would now call a nervous breakdown, and became the only person who dared prognosticate ill to Henry VIII regarding the Anne Boleyn crisis.

The Star and the Ditch

1

A scholar passed this way, in the dark autumn
Of tradition, lodged in the house you see –
Was commonly heard to hope for a night
Free of clouds, his haggard man unloading,
For observance of the 'angels' country'.
Through glowering pipe-smoke, the folk saw him
Robed in piety and city self-regard,
A discovery of foreign linens, between
Puckered bowls of vinegar, cabbage-hearts –
But liked the sound of his coins in their brass.
'Let him open his charts to the wind, if he wants,'
They said. 'Let him follow his comet's course,
Pay his money, be forgotten.'
Having eaten, out he went, case in hand,
His man blinking by the unstowed luggage.
As he passed, the candles shook their elfin heads.
Laughing, he would be back for the next meal.
But when hours had passed without return, they feared him robbed, or dead.

They came upon him that morning, at dawn,
His gear all bent, spun out of reach,
Frightened hands upstretching from the ditch.

2

The earth's curve is not visible from here,
This distance; you must be further away,
So the horizon can no longer be seen.
So with this moonstruck man. Year by year,
Orion's flesh developed in his eye
Like a fevered death-bed scene
Painted when he passed the test of birth.
I wonder how he shivered through his death –
Crooked as a stick in shallow water,
Chest ragged in moonlight, anti-matter
Invisible to the seraphic lens –
Making sense

Of a map of silence. Scream of a night-bird.
Do you see him, this gooseflesh shambling towards the last word?
Or, stopping, see the lamps of a flooded town
Trembling in ditch-water, and make to touch,
Sleeves rolled to the elbows, forearms wet,
The pith of what you can't quite yet make out:
Branches raised, defying the starry ditch.

Ekphrasis

The men with pipes and braces lean
Like cornstalks frozen in a trench.
Their pint-pots glitter, damascene;
Victoriana; serving-wench;

It's cardboard 1849
In Jarrow (not a golden year)
And workers from the local mine,
Arraigned with beer, in grainy air,

Pose to make the camera smile.
The acids of the pig-iron age
Sharpen into skin: no Sheol
Scrubbed and cleaned to make a stage –

These people were not actors. They,
Like orators of ancient Rome,
If they could speak, would, nodding, say,
'The rule of law begins at home.'

My friend and I discuss 'Guernica',
Goya, Edvard Munch's 'The Scream',
The church in P— where swastika
And cross are meshed and co-blaspheme

Against the wall – dear God! – the sight
Of industry from various quays –
The slant dawn-wire unpicked by light –
The new town. Furnished factories.

I turn away to drink, and rest
My flickery reflected head
Against the window: palimpsest:
Crowded bar-room; flower-bed;

And then we are outside, agreed
(And drunk) that pictures never lie.
Those flowers, like a people freed,
Would nod us to complicity.

Judas

St Swithin's Day,
you kissed me on the cheek
I'd turned
to the luxury of sunbathers
gaggling there to see
if I would vanish
in a puff of holy smoke.
O Adonai,
I vanished in a trice –
root now among the skulls
of that many-headed beast,
a torrid pulse:
discretion's soul,
so good they damned him twice.

And on the wall
to the hibiscus kingdom
stood a sign
sprayed up by some benign
malingerer

(no doubt)
by now long gone
beyond the far gates with their nodding plumes of sun;
while I, small soul,
orbited the halo of your head –
my one fiducial point –
not god, not man, not bird
nor beast nor plant
IF U CAN READ THIS YOUR ALREADY DEAD

my blood inflaming at your pulse,
my pulse your blood
and thunder
bringing on the cold sweat of rain
at noon
as shadows branched across your face.
The paths are straight
(I'm told)
on which we meet,
we whistlers in the dark,
the ones we will forsake.
Now, open your unearthly eyes and start –
as though a ghost of heaven
puffed against your cheek.

A Letter from Polème

This Year of Good God 1790 (blighted
be its annal!) year of common
rule, uncommon riot; the old ways rutted-at,
untenable, I rode southward
to Polème. Three days of cold (writing without light)
three nights, saddle-weary, well passed.
How slowly came I here! How masterfully kept
my back straight on the straight road back
to Hell – such wrought enormities housed in this place! –
dreaming of the green walks to come,
his gardens rustling rustic fictions in my brain.

The Count coddled me in rich wine.
I watched him lace the air and palated my quiet,
movement being air made flesh, flesh
unspeakable. Like an anxious shade, the candles
cast me on his lordship, arranged
thereon the wight of his lost house, an alien
cadenza playing on itself
(Nota, the question of the sum is yet unfixed
&c. &c.
the Count is more distrait, abstracted, these last days –
if this seems strange I am sorry)

He admires my selflessness and confessed as much;
I confess in faith, coming to
his point of view, I admire him for saying so.
Quixote of your riven sky,
O Moon! Enmantled yet, my comprador of light!
For I would not alert my host
to this my writing – there is a weird, subtle wire
binds me to this blasted helix,
a thing of Youth with scant attachment to the world
taking account of dead money.

(Tempered in the hissing wine, the will – iron, but hot –
is forged and bent. See! in the glass
grows a dawn of iron, as wine passing hot through blood;
as through a washed-up, half-drowned wretch.
Dribbling white sand, he dreams himself a golden mouth.
Yet politicking with the Count,
I count myself, of late, with the dreamers, lying
earth-hooked, tracing his lineaments
on ruin'd cloud)

For what dim purpose came I so
slip-shoddy into Hell? Through purpose, accidence,
I am quite utterly absorbed –
his kindness adversarial compels me here –
the Oleanders spike my heart
like Opium – the Count coddles me, holding me
in usufruct as in rich wine
(writing in the dark is seldom easy, my friend)

Jericho

Funnily enough there's only air
between us, no wall
of monumental moment and renown
to storm at, blow up or bulldoze down,
nor lock to twist off with the minor key of song;

though for some reason – as you mark well –
I've brought along
my own wall-flattering trumpet to blow
with one desire, to enter Jericho.

Of Scaurus, a Rich Man and Covetous

(after Tito Strozzi)

They should rename this rotten little town
'Scaurusville', so much of it you own,

Scaurus. You've all there is to have –
Mistress Moneybags your pale, leather-booted love –

Yet hook and crook for more, with a hunger
Worthy of hell's most accomplished beggar,

Slug-bellied! Yet, take a total nobody
Like Fabricius, if you can: it is he

Who is the richer man, delving in his field
Of hard labour where profit will not yield

To plump, powdered hands; for you do not own
Him, Scaurus, though you run this rotten town.

Epitaph on Elizabeth Barton, the Nun of Kent

Close to your king (close enough
to share some light) stuffed

into dark pockets of earth, a love
preserved, soiled remnant of a ragged love

thrown down and sky
inclement as an English prophecy:

the chisel etching loud and clear
the silence you cannot but hear.

Kensho River

Stepping across the river, Huang Po
caught himself reflected in its glass.
A white horse with black mane, upside-down,
trailed its dray; a hen corralled her chicks
into the engulfing pool of sky.

Huang Po was closer to that water
than a paper rose. He saw himself
awash with moss, the stream bright with cloud –
his body drawn backward from the rock
like Chicken-and-Egg, like Cart-and-Horse.

from Four Versions of Borges

'Yo'

The skull unseen, the heart invisible,
the motorways and byways of the blood
I cannot fix, inconstant as the god
Proteus, all nerves, guts, bones; as physical

as change itself, I am these things. And yet –
I am, too, the memory of a scimitar
slicing down the sun, and a blood-red sunset
turning grey, and darkening, and a single cellular star.

Lookout on the world's shore, I see the ships
endlessly replanked. I am the numbered books
and letters thin with time, the dry codex,
words mouthed indecently by long-dead lips.

Stranger, even, are these words I write
in a room somewhere, full of dust and light.

Mina Gorji

My poems respond to and investigate the strange and sometimes darker side of nature; poisonous plants, fruit-fly mating, weeds, slugs, wasps' nests. I am drawn to things that might seem ugly or rebarbative but, on closer inspection, have their own beauty and intricacy. Often a poem begins with information, found in a book or conversation, a fact which has a resonance or a cadence which makes it stand out. Something has to happen to turn this into a poem, something strange and unpredictable, a process of calm and obsessive tinkering, from which sounds and patterns emerge and gather into shape. Sometimes I start with an end in mind and work backwards; often I don't know where the poem will end up. Change is one of the subjects I return to in my writing; transformation in the natural world, but also in people's lives. In oblique ways perhaps some of the poems explore my own experiences of transition, moving, when I was a small girl, from a revolution in Iran to a calm suburban England. I love subjects that escape: Houdini, the bittern's cry, dandelions proliferating across whole continents, the reincarnation of a seahorse into aphrodisiac, people and things facing up to limits and moving beyond them – by ingenuity or art.

Forbidden Fruit

My first batch
of Poplar-cap, -
lightly fried,
on toast,
made me hesitate.
Dangers of the delicate:
the Deadly webcap
(easily confused
with Chantarelle)
or Avenging Angel
whose pale green cap
can kill,
the glycosides
in Bluebells
and in Buttercups
that blister skin
and make the heart
erratic,
and hemlock
that's so easy to mistake
for Parsley, Fennel,
Lady's Lace.

Empire of the Dandelion

Blowball, Puff-Ball, *pis-en-lit*,
Priest's Halo –
Sin in the Grass,
one tiny spore
proliferates –
an empire spread on air; dandelion –
blown across the oceans by ill winds,
weed and bitter remedy –
chicoria, pissabet,
bittera tzelaut.

Bittern

it thrives
in brackish water
where the sea has broken in –
in marshes and on river banks –
edges of solid ground.
When danger comes
it imitates the reeds
sticking its head up straight
and swaying in the wind.
A nervous bird, more often heard than seen,
its hollow boom
was heard at night
in ancient and in empty times –
in Nineveh and Babylon.

Kamasutra (the subsidiary arts)

To make designs
on courtyard floors
with ricepowder and sand
is seventh of the sixty four
arts to hold desire.
Cutting patterns
out of leaves
is number five.
Forty-third
teaching minah birds
and parrots how to talk.
And if you master repartee,
sign language, foreign tongues,
and practise all these arts of love –
there's no room left
for emptiness,
no time
for broken hearts.

Serenade

The female fruit fly cannot sing
but she can recognise
the warm vibrato
of a mate:

a serenade
not issued from the tongue –
but from the high-pitched trill
of hidden wings;

if clipped
he grows invisible
to her. They can collide a thousand times
inside this glassy chamber,

but caught
in unnatural silence
she is insensible,
and bears no fruit.

Be consoled

the wind transforms to rustling,
the sun to coal,
the coal to smoke and cinder flakes, –
the deepest lakes evaporate
and, raining, only seem to break
the fragile moon.

Reincarnation

Its coronet
distinctive
as a thumbprint,
the seahorse –
Hippocampus–
shares – or rather gave – its name
to a tiny part of human brain
located on the floor
of the lateral
ventricle,
that governs short
term memory
and spatial navigation.
Slow-moving,
and a poor swimmer,
it relies
on camouflage
to escape
reincarnation
as paperweight
or souvenir.
With luck, perhaps,
it might,
dissolved
into a tonic
against human
impotence,
be born again
with legs.

Night Garden

Late at night the slippered feet
move stealthy over torchlit grass.
The night air gathers into dew,
the silver scissors hunt out slugs.

Light shines through the bean leaves –
They're perforated into lace;
pearlescent tracery appears,
and here and there
bright snips of jet.

The art of escape

The great Houdini closed his eyes.
Imagining himself
inside the lock –
iron passageways
opened before him.
He felt his way along these dark canals
and out of a coffin
submerged in water,
or from a straitjacket, buckled
and suspended from a bridge,
like a giant man-moth.
Closing his eyes
he felt the night air
close against his skin:
even the outside
couldn't hold him long.

Pitseolak

I draw what I have never seen –
the monsters and the spirits,
the old ways,
and how we lived
before the white men came.

I travelled in a boat
with sails
made from the intestine of whale,
and fished for halibut
with silver hooks,
and hunted caribou.

I came to recognise
the gainful loss –
and could interpret
all its sounds –
the questioning
of birds at sea,
the crack of ice,
the coming thaw:

living a life
between these shores –
I, born inside a sealskin tent,
hear on the radio
two men have landed on the moon.

Pearl Diver

'Young women today don't like the sea as much as we do, they lack courage and don't want to get their skin darkened by working in the water.'

Kotoyo Motohashi, *Pearl Diver or 'Ama'*

Upturned
fishing boats –
cormorants
dry their wings.

An empty tub
for abalone,
cuttlefish,
or octopus
settles on the woodblock waves.

One long breath
and Kotoyo descends,
like her mother
and her grandmother
before her.

Currents stir the kelp;
water murkens:
Kotoyo
can barely see her hands –

or the knife
that separates
sea-bed from oyster shell.
She is last of the Ama
of Shirahama.

Arto Vaun

A boy presses his face against a storefront in 1980 in Watertown, MA. Dusty glass and late summer shadows. There are jars full of rocks. It's a small office, closed for the weekend, though it always seems closed. The boy knows this because he lives upstairs with his grandparents during the summer. It's an old large burgundy house, built around 1900, right next to Mount Auburn Cemetery. On hot afternoons his grandmother chases him around in the large kitchen, and they laugh. His grandfather listens to the news and looks at atlases while drinking Miller High Life. Somehow, the boy knows that this is magic.

Years later, the house is a parking lot. That's it, just a parking lot. Like many things in the boy's heart, flattened without a trace. Was it ever really there? Turns out, it doesn't really matter. What matters is that the boy has learned how to take words, like rocks from a jar, and build things. He builds shelters for the lovely ghosts around him. He builds and rebuilds loss into futures. Some people call it poetry. He calls it home.

My Father's Sleep Was Never a Blueprint

I come back to this machinery
This dark cologned compartment

I come back to wool sports jacket
Rickety door and silver watch

I put out my strange hand
Into the breath you keep taking back

Stubborn with your closed eyes
Shut like caves no one knows are there

The corridor you'd pass me in
The corridor where you were tired

Comes back the wall-to-wall carpeting
That took our steps absorbed our weight

Made us all beige in that house
Lulled possibility into drywall

The joists between floors noticed
Something pressing down

The timber I come back to
From 1910 a derailed past

Where rain gets in sometimes
Turns its entrance yellow turns

Our eyes to it we try everything
To keep it out

Father and Son in Orbit (July 1969)

I am done talking about the moon – its lit body
Does not caress, does not notice even the few
Footsteps being left there right now, weightless crushes
Upon its cold skin, its zero memory, austere
Imprints that will remain precise in their loneliness
Far, far past us, sitting here – father, son, static
On the television mimicking our locked insides

As audience, we are perfect – facing forward, speaking little
And well dressed, even for this, even in our own home
Your pale hands adorned with age spots, adorned
With a solidity and conviction I fear to comprehend
Just as perhaps you fear yourself randomly, alone in bed

A scratchy voice from the pathetic dark distance
Reaches our living room, falls to the floor from gravity

Capillarity I

America, now I will try it this way:
All my years, after all, are bursting yellow-blue on this day
And I am walking as we all have walked on pavement and roads
Treading on each other's struggling skin-souls
                    Trampling without knowing any better

Our towns are forgetful and we are only human though we have built
And burned down – we toss and turn in our sleep and wake up grumpy

So let them come forward, who cannot see straight
Let them come forward, who are on fire, all crackling heat
Let them come forward, whose knees are those of a wounded elk
Let them come forward, who have been nudged off the map
Let them come forward, who have forgiven and cry while driving

Let them come forward, who smell the cut grass and the wound around
the corner
Let them come forward, who are my kin, your kin, and there when our
hands sweat

Is it possibly in the way the finch flew close to my sun-veiled face
When I was so close to home –
It took something with it from me as I felt the weight of its wings
Maybe something I wanted taken

Forget everything you know, I told myself, because you have started
To see glimpses of what it is really that inches toward you
Like a cluster of sparkling universes in a baby's palm
That you take to your lips

I was so close

Capillarity XXVIII

A violinist loved my mother he would have done anything for her
But that was not what she wanted she wanted to fight it
Fight any possibility of life-on-skin happiness that would be messy
And embarrassing what would people say so she married
My dad when she got to America and she did love him
Eventually I learned to love him she said and I believe her
Because when he slumped over and died at his friends' house
My mother came apart like a bursting bubble like Lego like glass
That's when I knew that she could love something madly in a way
That she did not seem to offer me it startled me seeing
Her on the mauve sofa like that all wet porcelain and cracked
Surrounded by impaired family and a lazy-eyed priest whose breath
Stank with the business of it all just as we stank in that living room
All together and not

Capillarity XL

Tonight there is a path under your feet
The owl shimmers and asks nothing of you
Somewhere a ship makes noise against dark water
Your parents have a memory you cannot begin to know
        See your moonlit hands

Tired of suspecting, tired of being suspect
You clamor like a rabid groupie to have a moment
Where someone else allows you
Just allows you
        To be a mess on this earth

Grandmothers everywhere, the children falling
Asleep in your arms under your bad breath
Will eventually want nothing more
Than to become that breath
        When they are all grown and choking

We cannot connect the dots or the bones
We cannot make it better with a kiss or sweater
The lemon is the suck of language in your cheeks
A paper cut on your tongue
        That you keep tasting as you walk

Capillarity XLI

One day you will arrive at the door
Crusted pale with mud, dry, noiseless
The cough in your heart will tangle itself
Like the fingers of your father at his wake
Tangled the way cells build us, then go

Once, you were unable to sleep alone
But once asleep you were alone as a vase
On a high oak shelf in your grandparents' apartment

Where one is a ghost now
And the other carries around too much in her purse
    She who is often ignored and knows it
    She who is still an orphan-girl on a riverbank
So far from pale you

Oh, how shall we explain it –
There is an elegant difficulty in breath
Just as a heavy airplane flying makes little sense
Or just as the silverback at the zoo gazes and gazes
We are falling so fast it feels still as sandstone

But please, tell me a story anyway
Tell me about the color green and much kissing
Sing me an aria and don't mind the language
It will mind you soon enough

Now, come in

Capillarity XLII

When you wake each morning you are waking up on earth
You are waking up on rubble, relativity, rhetoric

Pulling the drapes open there it all is, your neighborhood –
Construction, messy dreams, bickering, awkward sex, pets

What do you mean when you shower – there is your body
Naked – you touch it the same way and are often disappointed

Last night there was a dream unraveling in your head like a gift
It offered itself the way a street thinks of you just as you turn onto it

There were people gathered around a dining room table all
Speaking over each other, almost Pentecostal

Pausing to look at you they dropped to a whisper
You wanted to have a seat, join them, be joined

This is what you can remember standing under the hot water
Some of it gets into your mouth and you don't mind

You think *water is in my mouth just as I am in the water*
Nothing dissolves when you think like that

Capillarity XLVI

Mother, it's so late in the North Sea air – your son's body
Is lit by faint city light, slouched against the past, soft-lipped

Look how his leg twitches, wants to get going, reach
The word *family* again, as though such a thing ever was

Migration doesn't allow you to fathom these words
And that has been our ocean spread silver between us

For years we have been fighting language, tidal
Wave after tidal wave punching air

From our mouths, leaving no room for a deep breath –
That is what being rootless is – wading up to our necks

Dazed after a flood no one saw coming
Our feet barely touch the earth under the thick water –

All the way from here, I can see you
Someone's mother, soaked, thin as a glass stem

Pummeled by history and unbelonging –
I want to say you shouldn't be afraid

Though the water is endless and loud
Though it scatters us

You shouldn't be afraid
I can see you from here

Capillarity XLVII

They have never been on a ship before, let alone
Anything called *sea* – 1947
And Beirut is, like them, dumb about the dense future
Already attaching itself like a cataract

Just passengers and waves – a little girl's hand
Slipping in and out of her 18-year-old mother's

Two hands, the world on that boarding plank
The sound of shuffling feet in some kind of counterpoint
With the echo of water and the dry swallow in throats

Partial moon sheds what it can – father and grandfather
Talk little, feel their ribcages are lit from the inside

Having made this decision and now, stepping off land,
One or both of them sense control spinning away
Like an angel tired of having to watch

The boarding plank bends from the future, arms
Clutching arms clutching whatever they can carry
Voices consumed by the in-between place, a small crevice –
Even in the most tenuous hand-holding there is
Still more warmth than the most glaring sun
                    About to come

Everyone sits where they can as though at mass
And the off-white ship begins to creak like a song
                    No one has heard before

Capillarity L

Then one day all the lights turned on they came
At the one who was lost came like the eyes of wolves

Standing there as in a fable thoughts were made
From construction paper and the one who was

Lost heard the paper being cut by the hands
Of children who were being cut

By the hands of the future our disheveled teacher
This kind of thing happens

Old men and women asleep know all about it
As do their shy pets and quiet silverware

The one who was lost had survived being
Lost for that is all that can be done

Caught in that electric white light cousin
To suns moons nervous wrecks among us

What is there an alibi two dangling
Hands at one's side and half-sight

Digging at your chest is useless
There is nothing there that is not out here

Capillarity LIX

Comes a time when all it takes is all missing
From the frame from the lens itself
There's no mechanism for it anymore

If you were to bend backwards to really look
Into the past the way the past looks into you
The river would not be so stubborn

How many times has spring gathered itself
In our towns and hearts making us believe
That somehow things will be different

Let me tell you this: a granular surface
Against your palm is the loveliest way home
Like the pages in the middle of a book or a stone

Once there was the person you were face
Against the glass the road ribboning by
While your father drove your mother sang

Your brown eyes become wet from the sun
That you were told not to stare at
Saturated with light and what we are to become

Capillarity LXII

Some call it the past an ember
There it is a hot song on your palm
No matter how you look at it it looks
Away

I should not have left
What choice did I have what
Other steps could I take all the lights were on
In the house but not in my father's body

So I walked in took the stairs was led
To a family melting on mauve furniture
Looking at me like the last inch of the last
Strand of light on a winter day yes I remember

My mother's eyes two lanterns way out in a field
How soft black the soil was our mouths became
Full of it so we gagged so we had only
These eyes of ours what could we do

This is the sound of denying whatever forgiveness
Owed me I'd rather you have it I'd rather you
Unclench finally see your hands they are warm they are
The miracle of holding anything at all

Capillarity LXVI

Until what this is sliced into what I have been until
I came out of the woods of your house the ponds
Of your dank pasts licked at my ankles singing

What was lost fell out of my kid-hands year after year
Half submerged and all the kingdoms let it remain so
I pled for whatever sunlit talk or hint of dry earth

Only your sorry mouths were dry and aimed like crossbows
At whatever flickered in the reeds it was my body there too
Still punctured this is how I woke up

David C. Ward

I started writing poetry in my late thirties and I think my poems show the influence, for both good and bad, of my education and occupation as an historian who works at a museum. I'm happy with them but they seem observational and maybe over-intellectualised and stiff. It's only rarely that I seem able to dissolve the wall of self-consciousness and write something more fluent; 'Still we pretend at modesty', for instance, which I think is about my best. In 'The Poet', Emerson advocated that writers use drugs and other substances to free up their minds and merge with their subjects. Not quite sure I'm ready for that but I do wish I had learned to dance when I was a teenager. On the other hand, 'know yourself!', as someone once said, so perhaps I can make a virtue out of my necessities. Regardless, I am pleased that I did start writing verse, especially since it seemed to come out of nowhere at a difficult time. I'm happy to accept the mystery and not question it too closely.

Def: Extreme Rendition

Rendition

'The handing over of a fugitive
Or some other party
Of interest to the duly constituted
Authority of the State
Or his representative.'

Rendition

A surrender; a submission:
A bringing –
To the knees.
A bagging of the head
And eyes – the state
Of nullity.

Rendition

Sing me the song
That's why you're here
Give me the stuff
We want to hear.
Spiel me the tune boy
And you might
Stay o.k. but you know
What happens
If you don't want to play.

Render

Tear skin from flesh
Break bone
Break
And boil, reduce to grease.
Re-heat. Repeat
As necessary and desired.

Render

Unto Caesar –
Or eat the thorns –

Render

End Here. Enter Here.

Colossus

He knew what he knew
and did not know
what he did not know
which was
America.

The city
The hill
The river:
all a blank
in his one eyed mind.

His voice silted
the city's streets
flattened the hill
stilled the river flow
to his gray resolve.

The bread
no longer the body.
The wine
no longer the body.
The body

no longer the body.
The horn's bell
mute, full of dry
and bitter
fruit.

He knew what he knew
and did not know
what he knew
was not
America.

The End of History

The knife, worn, sharpened to a mercy,
Poised tight on the son's jugular,
The neck offered, right knee pushing
The boy's back, left hand cupping
The boy's eyes, pulling back
Against the knee braced in the
Boy's back. Eternity holds the pose.

Sun sliding down, time starts:
The father's eyes filling with salt
The boy pissing himself
The knife slipping
Slicing a shark red wake
To splash the naked rock.

Where is the Angel now?

The River Refuses its Name

On the 400th anniversary of Henry Hudson's discovery of the Hudson River

The river was the river's before it was ours.
Pull back and see it as it was. Reverse the flow
Of time and unpeel our landscape from the land.
Take the names and maps away: the incised grid
Of highway, road, and bridge; the connective tissue
That gives a motion to our lives. Take away the imprint
Of the names we give to place and time:
This landmark, or that battle,
This statesman or that conglomerate
From overseas. The markings that we make
In all our ceaseless commerce in the world. The walls
Of glass, the city's tunnels warrened underground,
And the restless bedlam shriek of all the dailiness

That keeps our lives afloat in what we know
As life. Modern times canyoning its heedless way
Through all our pasts and all we think we can control.
So thus the reassurance that we get from naming things
To get some fictive grip on all we think we've learned
Or know, a sense of where we've been and where we go,
The habitual views that we pass by each day
Distracting us in custom's groove and rote
From what is now and what we've never really seen.

                    So start over. Think beyond ourselves
This time and all that we kept out by all our putting in.
Go back to see the river as it was before we started time.
Don't think of the river as ourselves.
Don't think of the river as our history.
Don't think of the river as anything but the river:
Cold, whole, inviolate, merciless in the integrity
Of its ceaseless mountainous riverflow.

Still we pretend at modesty

These days, dreams of modest heroism
cloud even the smallest tyrant's mind.
Who is exempt from self-effacing hubris?
No one is an erratic driver or a bad lover
when history is behind the wheel of fate.
We can't kid ourselves; we all acquiesce.
Everything is in play now as even quiet
moments down by the old mill pond
are a product placement opportunity. But
still we pretend at modesty even as we rise
like trout to plaudits which sting our mouths
with the ashes of electronic funds. Rinse, repeat:
was any complex civilisation ever founded
on such a simple formulation?

So, Katy bar the door.
And if you're doing nothing tonight, please drop by?
We'll each keep a foot on the floor, like pool players,
and keep company for a while. You won't stay.
Who does these days? One (notice the distancing
pronoun) gets used to it. Yet alone or not, sometimes
in the waking dream of night, cutting the electric
chatter which now hums our synapses, I smell white
water and follow the tracery of rivers among cold pines.

No Place

It's hard to fathom anymore
with no more news from nowhere.
Quiet nostalgia is a frail reed to justify
lives lived to the rhythm of t.v. dinners
and traffic reports. The verities of weather
trouble us only on video while our lives
seal us up with air-born mites and molds.
Where did all these lung ailments come from
anyway? The pine scented fresheners
don't seem to work and wearied
by the ersatz sublime desperate measures
are required. At least by some.

Poor heart: no more Aeolian
strings humming the hyperbolic ether, a dynamo
gorgeously electrifying us in all our struggles
and up against which we were fierce in losing.
Now the thrum is all inside while our internal air
crusts up canals and channels, rimes our tear ducts
shut with salt. Erratically, a recurring dream breaks
through halcyon day nights of sleep: A river
shimmers just beyond that near-distant scrim of trees.
So close, we could almost walk there if we would.

Surplus Value

My Michigan brother-in-law was a tool and die guy,
A machinist, fabricating parts in shops supplying Big Three
Auto makers. A bantam with thick fingers, scarred hands
He rode a Harley soft-tail, drank Iron City, and lived
With his wife and kids in a house he mostly built himself.
During the heyday of Detroit metal, overtime and union
Contracts paid for steaks and a cabin on an upstate lake
For summer vacations and deer season hunting trips
In the fall. He took his pride from his craft and skill
Building something bigger than the Fords or Chevys
He pushed on down the line for America to drive.
For twenty years of work, good times, and happy with it.
But that road ran out. The union went south first
(pension fraud; indictments; prison terms) and then
The companies and their money men slashed and burned
Their way through labor and its costs in search of market
Share. The work was sweated from the men for less and less return.
From economy of scale, to one of scarcity: subcontracting, piecework,
Ultimately the dole replaced a steady pay check and a bonus
Twice a year. The Harley went and then the cabin; food stamps
Bought essentials, nothing more. Always quiet, he grew quieter
From day to week to month to the years that stretched ahead,
Bowing his neck each day as the scars grew deeper now, and inward.

During the boom that no one thought would ever end,
Heedless the factories flushed their waste straight into
The Saginaw River, so much so that it never iced, even
In the depths of winter. Now it's frozen all year long.

Relict

My great aunt Carlie (from Carlton, her family name)
despite Parkinson's and widow's weeds lived to be one hundred
and four years of age. Born in the Centennial year, 1876
she passed away in 1980, living alone in the Danvers Home
for the Aged and Infirm having outlived two husbands
(the first died in the 'flu epidemic of 1917, the second in 1952),
sons and daughters, assorted collateral kin, even her younger
sister, who only made it to ninety-four. Every Fourth of July
for a long time she rode in the town's Independence Day
parade, honored as Danvers' eldest citizen. A bright spark
to near the end and something of a ham, she loved waving
to the crowd from the back of a big boat Cadillac convertible,
the one with shark-like fins. As she aged her mind refused
to focus on the here and now but she kept a startling vision
of her father's sad decline from wealth to someone in the trade:
a disastrous turn of the century decision to back kerosene,
not gasoline. A not unfamiliar history, status thereafter derived
not from money or striving but from lineage: A family
and its place in time. Avid for genealogy she traced her family –
Putnams mostly – back to the Bay Colony, the Covenant, the
City on a Hill and all the history that could be spun out from
those first things. A teleology of grace and consolation
as the world passed the North Shore by. Her family – mine too –
had a window in Fanueil Hall, graves in the Old Granary,
were patriots who fought in one or another revolutionary battle
(the details were always somewhat imprecise) and formed
the backbone of the DAR and the Cincinnati, those momento
morii of a declining race. She never moved far from
those little towns, satellite to Boston's hub, sitting still
and calm as time washed in from somewhere else and left
her looking back, with a clearer sense of where it was she'd been.

Aces and Eights

Early mornings, two or three a.m., when my father couldn't sleep
He'd make his way downstairs and brew a coffee, black and bitter
To sit at the kitchen table with a pack of Luckies and a deck of cards,
Dealing out dummy poker hands, playing them himself against himself.
Five or seven card stud were his games; never draw, a game for kids,
He'd say, not a real man's game. Calculating odds and chances in his head,
He'd check and raise, hold and fold, spinning cards out in semicircular
Array to put them through their paces. Smoking all the while and sipping
From his cup, he'd impose his pattern on their random fall of meaning.
He'd learned to play, like most of the men of his generation, on football
Roadtrip bus rides and then continued in the War, breaking the monotony
Of hurry up and wait with an endless game of table stakes with cash
That it was bad luck to keep, a smaller gamble of one's luck against
The biggest cashing out of all. Cutthroat camaraderie that men learn
To relish, the poker games didn't long survive once middling age,
Professional aspirations and ultimate success, domesticated affluence
(a wife; three kids) took up all his time: no waiting now, all hurry.
Now dealing out the dummy hands was a vestigial routine, a way to fight
Another war, against the daily rote, the clock, and what he thought
He had become. A mindful mindlessness in which the fall of pasteboard
Squares filled the night's unease, keeping out the growing sense
That something somewhere had been lost somewhere back in time.

★

Outside the old Victorian in which we lived, the sky would begin to
lighten,
He'd let the dogs out (they were his wife's in truth), and clean the ash tray
and coffee cup,
Taking time with rituals, filling each necessary day.

Clothes Make the Man

After my father died the chores
    of death were done
until nothing but his clothes
    remained. I stood,
my mother out walking with the dogs,
    at his closet going
through a life in cloth. From fifties'
    vanilla conformity,
demobilised khaki, academic corduroy,
    an ascending arc
of a career, gravitas stitched out
    in suits and ties
of finer text, more subtle hues; we
    buried him in his best.
And as the cloth rippled, bespoke waves
    under my casual hands
a flicker of greed licked out: we were
    at least I thought
same sized, why let such rich things waste?
    I admired a broadcloth
three piece banker's stripe up against
    my chest and as I did
I caught not just my father's overt scent
    of bay rum and pomade
but a tracery of something deeper, fine
    woven in the cloth.
I put the jacket at my face to unforewarned
    go under at the sudden
cordite stink of all his working life.
    Ambushed, I could
not breathe again until all the hangers
    swung like ruined gallows.

Two San Francisco Poets

Weldon Kees' Car

was found by a cop on the beat
at 2 a.m. in a park near the Golden Gate,
the doors and windows open, fog tendrils
blowing – an easy metaphor picked up
by literary detectives trying to fathom
Kees' unexplained, shocking vanishing.
The law assumed suicide or 'death by misadventure',
empty car plus proximity to the suicide bridge
added up to a familiar story. Case closed. But no
body was ever found and years later a journalist
claimed to have seen Kees somewhere down
in Mexico – probably in the same town where JFK
hangs out with Marilyn and Elvis (slim again) plays
hillbilly guitar. The reporter said Kees ducked him
And disavowed all knowledge of the arts.
Other sightings have been made, all uncomfirmed.
Weldon Kees: painter, poet, specter of what
Might have been. When he got lost he had
A growing reputation. He desired none.

Jack Spicer

kept a bottle always handy to drown
the words that streamed incessantly
through him like the jolt from an electric chair.
A student of linguistic theory, he concocted
a theory – unprovable, disparaged, incomplete –
that we are but like radio receivers for a language
beamed in from somewhere else. A passive
antennae, he tried to order all the chaotic words
streaming through his appalled and unsuspecting
mind, an incessant fizzing overload that froze his will.
Gripped in a logos he could not comprehend,
he gibbered, spoke ecstatically. People shied away.
Tortured for years, he finally flipped the switch,
drank himself to death and at the end diagnosed
himself precisely: 'My vocabulary did this to me.'

Teleology

Wouldn't everything have been a lot easier
    if: Arriving at the terminal
the lovers missed each other, and wandered
    aimless in the crowds until,
one waiting in the bar, the other leafing magazines
    they both picked up casual
conversations with strangers which quickly moved
    with an audible click,
brushing a lock of hair, having a second drink,
    to something else, from which
brush contact they both danced slowly and then
    suddenly into long loves full
of children and delight. Thus forestalling the
    inevitable slow slough of boredom
and middle-class routine – ennui with adultery,
    outbreaks of broken crockery –
for which a dyspeptic not too attentive God marked them.
    So that years later both
tried to recall who it was they were to meet that day
    but gave up with a laugh
after a thought's flicker to make dinner and love.

Instead, time unrolled for them as for empires:
    drawn through the crowd
ineluctably they met and in a second fell.

William Letford

I was lucky enough to receive an Edwin Morgan Travel Bursary from the Arts Council of Scotland. This allowed me to spend three months in the mountains of Northern Italy helping to restore a medieval village. The poems in this anthology were written while working as a roofer in my home town, Stirling, and working in Italy, on the restoration of Baiardo.

They speak of the gods

He says Hades, and I see Richard, wearing his welding mask
kneeling beside a stripped out Citroen, sparks from his torch
lighting one side of the garage wall. She says Zeus, and I see
Casey, framed against the sky, bloated and happy
carrying cement across a tiled roof.

It's aboot the labour

hammers	nails
hammers	nails
hammers	nails

heh Casey did a tell ye a goat
a couple a poems published
widizthatmean
widayyemean
dizthatmeanyegetmoneyfurrit

eh	naw
aw	right

hammers	nails
hammers	nails
hammers	nails

By the time we met

Candlelight was kind to her. Her fork seemed
weightless, but seldom made the journey upwards.
I suspect that she had tasted asparagus before.
Conversations clashed around her and dispersed
like circles on the surface of a lake.
After the Shiraz, I had courage, and I said. *You
must have been something when you were younger.*
Quiet, so none could overhear, she touched
my arm and replied. 'We stumble into youth
by accident, from somewhere else, and spend
the rest of our lives making our way home.'

Moths

                                        Moths

        Moths

                Moths

fucking moths
perforated my kilt between weddings
larvae feeding   somewhere in the bedroom
wardrobe   under the bed   i don't know
heads full of light bulbs   and moons   erratic
fucking moths

        Moths

                        Moths

                        Moths

Taking a headbutt

your pal ruffled ma hat
i said, what? made the mistake of leaning forward
and that was that

blood-metal darkness and the taste of brass
the bell was rung
i know i went somewhere
because i had to come back

Waking for Work in the Winter

Even when frost hasn't left the hard ground rutted by the wheels of tractors
Even though tail lights clog the motorway
Even though the moon still stands blind and cold in the morning sky
Even though the sheets are clean and the covers are warm
And the person beside you breathes the rise and fall of somewhere deep
Get up
Like the dog that hears a sound in the dark
Get up

Winter in the World

The old lady struggles, footsteps careful, leaving shuffle marks in the snow.
No shopping bag, so maybe it's church, and maybe not. Perhaps she is out
for a walk, because she can, and the night is spare, and she is undiminished,
and harder than bone.

Sunday, with the television off.

I think of the future. My death bed. I imagine the man I will be. Then I
pay that man a visit. Ask him, what would you do?

So I leave the car and walk across town. Knock on my fathers' door to say
hello and listen to his stories, the ones I've heard before.

It's like I've travelled in time. Now he knows that someone is listening. On the
way home, the sun falls behind the buildings, and I walk into a supermarket.

In the Mountains of Northern Italy

The chapel on the hill has no roof. For five hundred years its four walls
have framed the universe. The locals laugh at the Sistine Chapel
and call it the coffin lid.

Working Away

Mornings are familiar. The heft of a still-saw. The weight of a drill. The
                                                                    texture
of rust. When to say yes, when to say lift it yourself. But the evenings are
                                                                    foreign.
The café in the piazza catches the sun at six. The waiter is openly bored.
                                                                    Workmen
drink wine, talk quietly, leave dust on the seats. Only the flies are busy.
                                                                    Yesterday,
the grocer gave me tomatoes for free. Most of them were half rotten.
So she used her thumb to show me where to cut.

Breakfast in Baiardo

the window to my right is open
and filled with mountains
that layer the distance until
there is almost no room for sky

the key hung by the door
has been stretched tight by gravity
pulled into place
every chair in the room is empty

the sugar bag crackles
and a line along the cooker tells me
that the ants   are on the march

Sunburst

one astronomical unit eight light minutes ninety three million miles
and right here bare chest top off beneath the sun god Ra
sweat beads arms ache heart pounding blue sky aware of my youth
aware of my strength above the noise of the street
a ridge to bed – a tile to repair – and the heat
one astronomical unit eight light minutes ninety three million miles
and right here

Worker

sweat the felt screed the cement
pack the joist level the cleat
eat the piece hammer the nail
                    string-line the future
                    raise the bones
                    build the skeletons
                    whistle the windows
                    into our rooms
                    hoist your brushes
                    sweep the sky

Impact Theory

It is 4:13 a.m. on New Year's Day 2010. My curtains are half closed.
Moonlight shows me the girl sleeping with her back toward me. She has the
outlines of stars tattooed onto her spine. Each one smaller until the void
beneath duvet makes it difficult to see. Tonight is the first time we've met.
With the tips of my fingers I touch the distance between the first two stars.
Then I halve that distance, and halve it again, and halve it again. Because
infinity isn't space and time, it's a process.

Helen Tookey

Sculptor Bruce Gernand writes, 'There is a need, not so much for clarity as for a clearing, a space where other orders of experience and meaning emerge.' This captures the way I think about poetry: each poem is a space, with its own particular form and dimensions and meanings, the latter generated partly by the poet and partly by the energies of language itself. One of the things I love about writing poetry is the way in which the form for a poem emerges, inseparably from the process of my working out what it is that I want to say – or rather, the process by which the thing that needs to be said works itself out through the poem.

I often write about places or landscapes and the pasts they contain or the way they 'hold' our heightened moments of experience or memory. Sometimes (as in the poem 'America') the place is somewhere I have never been, the poem a network of associations spiralling out from the physical word that is the place-name – which connects to a wider fascination with the nature of language, and the ways in which different languages shape different worlds.

Start with this gesture

Thus the first language in the first mute times of the nations must have begun with signs,
whether gestures or physical objects, which had natural relations to the ideas to be expressed.

Vico, *The New Science*

Start with this gesture: a flinging of the
hands, so. A casting-forward, it says *from*,
away, out. Palms upwards, *empty, nothing,*
gone.

    Recast the movement in your mind:
conceive with what economy, supple
and synoptic, you comprehend chaos –

the accidents of human life, passions,
foibles, fates, restated as mechanics
and geometry,

        though still, as for reasons
and motives, baffling as crazy Ares,
tail-chasing round our upturned bowl of sky.

Among Alphabets

We met among alphabets. I saw myself
Greek: walking the walls, inviolate
as logic, mistress of
philosophy's glassy tongue.
Translation came slow. I learned to trust
Hebrew's rich misreadings, risk breeding
between the lines: language
of faith, our leap in the dark.

At Burscough, Lancashire

Lancashire's Martin Mere was the largest lake in England when it was first drained,
to reclaim the land for farming, in 1697.

Out on the ghost lake, what's lost
is everywhere: murmuring in names
on the map, tasted in salt winds
that scour the topsoil, westerlies
that wrenched out oaks and pines, buried now
in choked black ranks, heads towards the east.
Cloudshadows ripple the grasses as the seines
rippled over the mere by night, fishervoices calling
across dark water. Underfoot, the flatlands'
black coffers lie rich with the drowned.

Prints

...within some strata the footprints of the animals, birds and humans frequenting the coast
at that time have been preserved... The females, often accompanied by children, would appear
to have been mainly occupied with gathering food, e.g. shrimps, razor shells
and other seafood. At one site there was a wild confusion of children's footprints
as though they had been mudlarking...
Gordon Roberts, 'The Lost World of Formby Point'

I

Patience you need and a strong back for digging
razor-clams, wheedling them up with salt and
tugging them out, blind snouts curling. Bored, the
children play catch-me-if-you-can, eeling
from each other's muddy hands, filthy and
shrieking with laughter. Minding the tide and
uncertain sky, sifting for shrimp, you try
to keep count: no little ones lost in the
creek or sneaking away to the hunting.
What you need's eyes in the back of your head.

II

Like two voices shifting into pitch, our
coastline after four thousand years maps yours.
Your fen and creek are gone, you wouldn't know
this fine sand drifted with pines; but here are
your mud-flats, become lithographic, and
here your people: four-toes, twisted, no use
at the hunt; this girl, months-heavy, inching
her way, clawed feet curled hard into the mud;
and the children, quick, unhurried, knowing
themselves alone possessed of the future.

Cockleshells

We are walking the littoral
of October, watching the tide

reach its decision. I carry
merely yesterday's meanings but

you are already translated,
turned towards the bright months while I

collect October's cockleshells,
curetted cleanly by the sea.

With Joe on Silver Street

Tuesday 1 August 1967
Said goodbye to Kenneth this morning. He seemed odd. On the spur of the moment I asked
if he wanted to come home to Leicester with me. He looked surprised and said, 'No.'

from the diary of Joe Orton

In scratty fake-fur jackets, jaunty caps
and baseball boots we saunter Silver Street,
skiving our *l*s: it's *Siu*ver Street to slack-
mouthed Midlanders like us, who can't be arsed
with alveolar laterals. Of course,
RADA and elocution did the trick,
but still you keep a hint of Saffron Lane –
it charms the pants off Peggy and the rest,
just like the coat: 'Cheap clothes suit me,' you smirked,
'It's cos I'm from the gutter'; and it works,
they're all down on their knees, lapping it up.
Sometimes I think I hate you, Joe: I can
be cruel, but cruelty is something pure
for you, a fire that kills and makes things clean
and true; and I know anger, but the rage
that shoots your star high through the London nights
is something I'm afraid to face. You've travelled
far beyond me, Joe, and you don't plan
on coming back, I know; but here we are
on Silver Street, and look, in black and white,
that little word you never had the time
to strike out from those last blind lines, Joe: *home*.

Estuarine

In the clear grace of dream I stood high
on the Edge, the wind tugging and the world
tumbling far below. Tiny lights signed
across the valleys and I knew, if I dived,
the icy sky would bear me

but I awoke at sea level, estuarine
and silted, caught seven years
at slack water, waiting
a turn of the tide.

In a Richer Mine

By Parma, on the flood-plain. The river,
in spate, dragging ochre under dirty

nails. Submerged a child, you resurface a
doll: mechanical eyelids, face cauled &

streaked with slip. Thin cries from the attic, zinc
disc in the spine: *within this room she is,*

whose eyes I caused to be put out, but kept
alive. Mama, mama! In the village

the Scouse priest relishes his chthonic words,
smacking his chops as you, the five-months' child,

awake and clutch under my heart, digging
with half-formed fingers in a richer mine.

Climbing the Hill at Sunset

...before I had always taken the sunset and the sun as quite out of gauge with each other...
but today I inscaped them together and made the sun the true eye and
ace of the whole, as it is.

Gerard Manley Hopkins, *Journal*

We climbed past St Rhuddlad's
to Pen-y-Foel, the hill
not bare though but
rich with small lives.
Rabbits ran from your
high child voices, while
tiny wings creaked
and beat around us.
England lay blank
beyond the slate hills,
the whole world curving
into the west; and the sun,
true eye and ace,
commanded all.

America

Broad and smiling as a Sunday
rivermouth, impossible word

between us: *america*. Wide
and easy speech, argument smooth

and seamless as an egg. Half-tongued
I stumble through the station at

Stephansplatz, past memorials
to lost wars, and to the playground

in the beautiful gardens, where
I watch my children disappear

undisturbed: macht nichts, sie kommen
wieder zurück. America

is where we can never meet, though
we lived there together for years.

Dan Burt

The nine poems the editors have chosen here fairly represent what my poetry has been about and how it's made.

For example, 'Motes' is a sonnet about how string theory ('ST') might affect us. It uses common experiences, broadly defined, and traditional form, metre, rhyme and the normal speaking voice to convey how we might feel were ST proven, that though daily life would not change, everything we feel about the world and our rôle in it would.

The poem's octave uses images from nature ('make rock cloud', 'waves roll seaward'), mathematics ('or pairs threes'), human sexuality ('us strip less feverishly') and music ('Bach's harmonies') to question what effect ST would have on experience. The quatrain employs examples of lust ('peek over your belly'), music ('English Suite') and the sea ('ocean cooling') in reply. The concluding couplet's metaphors for the world and life ('blue pebble', 'a child's room') qualify that answer: the twist in the tail.

Clearly I believe, *pace* Adorno, there is little poetry cannot, in time, encompass. It exposes reality's heart, cuts experience whole and beating from daily life in a memorable, resonant, unsentimental fashion that remains after print is put by; at its best does in short lines what Auerbach and early Bacon did continuously in paint.

Un Coup de Des

Chance authors all we do,
The plot's contrived in retrospect.
Spied once I still look out for you;
Chance authors all we do.
A sea bird shot, a woman met
Ungloving who then strolls from view
Alters to fate as we reflect.
Chance authors all we do,
The plot's contrived in retrospect.

Who He Was

Joe Burt 1915–1995

I

He catapulted from his armchair,
airborne for an instant, primed to smash
the fledgling power who dared challenge
his rule. That runty five-year-old who would
not stop his catch to fetch a pack of Luckys
crossed some unmarked border, threatened
the kingdom's order and loosed the dogs of war.

No chance to repent, no strap, no bruises
on my face, my mother's screaming just static
behind the pounding taking place; rage spent,
sortie ended, he thumped down the stairs
to his crushed velvet base, pending new
provocations to launch him into space.

Worse followed till my biceps hardened,
but that first strike left most scars: with strangers
six decades on klaxons *ahwooga*,
the clogged heart hammers, I weigh my chance.

II

A scion of the tents of Abraham
born during World War I, he policed
a patriarch's long list of rights: no one
but he sat in the fat feather armchair
confronting the T.V. or at our table's
head, read the paper before he did or
said *Let's go somewhere else* when we ate out;
if he fell sick the house fell silent, roared
and we all quaked.

           I was chattel as well
as son and he sold my youth for luxuries:
an extra day a week to fish, lunch time
shags with his cashier, a kapo's trades.

My anger, like an old Marxist's, leached
away as parenthood, mistakes and time
taught Moloch is a constant. Attic myth,
Old Testament, bulge with sacrifical
tales, the Crucifixion one more offering
to Baal; families recapitulate
phylogeny, it's what some fathers do.

III

the golden land in the 'Thirties

Morning he threads russet gorges
of two-storey brick row houses,
short pants, pals, eighth grade
shut behind him, and evening
draggles home past trolleys full
of profiles who paid the nickel
he can't afford to ride

              no one
waits dinner: his mother leaves cold
soup in the kitchen (on Fridays
chicken) he gobbles by the sink
and chases with a fag puffed
on the way to box, while siblings,
older, younger, scribble lessons
or meet friends; sleeps alone

above the back porch in an unheated
room; wears his brother's hand-me-
downs; his father beats him bloody
for spending part of his first pay-
check on a first pair of new shoes

for cash he boxes bantam weight
before crowds shrieking *kill the kike,*
hawks sandwiches from wooden carts
to high school kids who once were friends,
at quitting time shoots crap with men
and at sixteen, meat hook in hand,
stands in a butcher shop's ice-box
breaking beef hindquarters down.

Depression shadowing the Volk
like a Canaanite colossus,
arms bent at elbows, palms turned up
hefts the male offering, sublimes
skin so it no longer feels pain,
fuses eyelids so rainbows shine
in vain, sears nerves so hands cannot
unclench and a decade on, when
ritual ends, amid ashes
the sacrifice survives, savage
more than man, hard, violent,
unbelieving, in the orbit
of whose fists lie his certainties.

IV

Bouts sometimes knocked him head to knees,
His swollen gut spewed crimson
Shit, he wasted until Crohn's disease
Left his great white hope the surgeon.

Clinched by tubes and drips post-op,
Missing most of his ileum,
Ribs prominent through cotton top,
Fed strained juice and pabulum
He went fifteen rounds with death.

The dark heavyweight danced away,
Doctors raised his wasted arm
And sent him south where snowbirds play
Hoping he'd recover weight and form.

There he eyed the champion
Crouched outside the ring to spring
Back for the rematch no one wins,
His belly's serpentine stitching,
The black before, the black after

And when again he spread the ropes
Apart, he could not see beyond
Himself and his ringside shadow.

V

The skeleton in a wheelchair props rented
tackle on the rail, stares down twenty feet
from a pier through salt subtropical air
at shoal water wavelets for blue slashes
flashing toward the bait below his float
and misses one hit, two, a third, an inept
young butcher far from inner city streets
recovering from surgery, too proud
to bask with codgers, too weak to walk or swim,
a sutured rag doll whose one permitted
sport is dangling blood worms from a pole.

His father's plumb and adze, mother's thread and pins,
tradesmen, carters, peddlers, kaftaned bearded
kin, village landsmen from Ukraine, friends, nothing
in his life smelled of ocean; but cleaver
held again, he kept on fishing. Once a week
he drove eighty miles east to prowl the sea
with charter-men, ever farther from the coast
till, white coat and meat hook junked, he trolled
ballyhoo for marlin eight hours run offshore.

Two score and four skiffs on, by his command
we laid him down in fishing clothes, khaki
trousers, khaki shirt, *Dan-Rick* on the right
breast pocket, on the left *Capt. J. Burt.*

Motes

Suppose it true Doctor Witten's strings
with ten dimensional flutterings
spawn numberless realities,
would that make rock cloud, or pairs threes,
us strip less feverishly
after months apart, Bach's harmonies
jar, waves roll seaward from a beach
to peak and break beyond eye's reach?

I'd still peek over your belly
to watch you bite your arm in frenzy,
wear out cds playing an English Suite,
sit by the ocean cooling sand-burnt feet

and yet, our blue pebble would seem smaller,
like a child's room now the child's older.

Trade

I

Barnegat inlet is a gauntlet
In the sea where waves break on sand
Bars that pen a bay, an unquiet
Place, lethal when easterlies stand
The long swells up to lumber
White capped across the shoals
And crumble in a khaki welter
Of seaweed, mud and spray that rolls
West through the cleft Atlantic coast.

II

Chartermen say little on the docks
At dawn standing by for parties,
For mates to ready boats – pull chocks,
Dog ports and stow necessities,
Bait, ice and beer – for copper gleam
To port ahead, gulls working gore
From sand eel shoals the stripers glean,
Or terns on blue fins hours offshore,
The world shrunk to a compass rose.

III

After noon the wind comes up, skippers
Go topside, shout *Reel in!* and head
For home; crews gut the catch, scuppers
Clog with viscera, decks turn red
Till seawater sluices them teak
Again and sunburned weekend
Warriors, beers wedged, peaked,
Doze and in day-dreams pretend
They're heroes home from the sea.

IV

Lines secured, the anglers leave
For row homes, showers, bowling club:
But by slips boatmen remain, reeve
Rod guides, observe the weather, rub
Penetrant on rusted pliers
And pause – to watch sedge sway on flats,
Geese rise honking from wetland choirs,
The sun decline, a whirl of gnats
And the Light flick on at Barnegat.

Indices

Measurement began braced against a kitchen jamb,
Head back, neck stretched like a young giraffe
Nibbling high leaves, waiting for the hand
Flattening my hair to notch my wooden graph,
And swelled into a hunger no nicked door
Satisfied. I shrank each milestone to size,
Schools and labours, lusts and loves, and scored
Them by league tables, money, conquests, wives;
A life, quantified.
                        Body marks me now
And I've had my fill of scores; but phthisis,
Shrinking bones, slack shank and jowl
Post the path to childhood's antithesis
No child can conceive, when with delight
It toddles toward evaluation and goodnight.

After Lunch

Mach two the green sign glows;
    You're far behind
Fifty thousand feet shows.
    And far below.

Crew start dinner service,
    We ate hours back,
Ask 'Scotch, soda, claret?'
    Our voices low.

Gladly I'd have missed this plane,
    Had you but asked,
To run with you again at dawn
    Hyde Park's pale rose lined paths.

Manqué

Through fog blown inland off the sea
By tumbled walls amidst old trees
Summoning verse from memory
That others wrote, I walk my land,
A stiff kneed quondam businessman
Fixed on Ulysses, lesser men,
Faded notes, a dry pen
    And fear, push come to shove,
    I am no good at what I love.

Sie Kommt

(...Es ist die Königin der Nacht...)
Tamino, *The Magic Flute* Act 1, sc. 2

She comes with a train of shadows never cast
By any earthly forms whose charge and mass
Thwart light; they flutter just beyond my grasp
Like cherry blossoms a puff of wind unclasps.

She comes around the corner of the years
Streaming faux memories from foreign piers
That never were, dreams I would clear
Of unshared passages, landfalls and tears.

She comes and, for a breath, regret recalls
An unmade voyage: our first-born's squall,
Trimming the sheets while teaching her to sail,
Her hand on mine before my father's pall.

Phantoms swimming in my deeps of night,
No magic flute can pipe you to the light.

Ishmael

Genesis 16:12

I

My father fished three days a week,
A maid helped mother clean and mend,
My brother's hands stayed soft and weak
And I was sent to the cold with men.

Swaddled in white coat chin to uppers
I trained from twelve to butcher meat
And dress it on enamelled platters,
Fat tucked like toes under bound feet;
Played Philoctetes to fowl bones,
Saw blue line crawl my ulnar vein,
Hied septic blood to wards alone
For antidote to purge the stain;
Made green meat red with dye and grinding,
Saw how back rooms broke men by fifty;
Stood behind a dumpster pissing
To save time when we were busy.

No angels graced that wilderness,
No wells, no Hagar, no augur
Sifting offal who foretold success
Beyond knife and block; no wonder
Drug for a child's mind gone tough,
No acne salve to hide the blush
When the father of a puppy love
Sniffed at the sawdust in my cuff.

Roots cankered past disinfection
I gave my back to home and nation,
An alien with alien vision,
Cancers present, though in remission.

II

A rusted ring bolt and long length of chain
Lie on the asphalt where a black dog prowls;
The hairless weal around its neck makes plain,
As well as spade ears, fangs, gun barrel snout
That this mailed compound long has been home.
Gates bear no warning; there's no need to snarl;
Scarred skin, the rasp while gnawing at a bone
Guarantee junked cars in near-by piles
Rest undisturbed and rot alone.

Identity

Come: do not touch me: let me alone discover
The holy and funereal ground where I
Must take this fated earth to be my shroud.
                    Oedipus at Colonus
                    (Grene and Lattimore eds.), ll. 1544–46)

I

Ego teeters on the tip of years
Honks a last horn, taps flippers, rears
To cheers and fish and waddles off,
An old thespian with a cough
Retreating to a circus cage
After a lifetime centre stage
To rot behind steel bars and wait.

II

Self examines the heap of time,
Hefts what is left, sifts all behind,
Gathers toddler tears, abiding pain
From rejection, not risked again,
Compacts the lot to stucco paste,
Concocts history out of waste
And plays Macaulay with your life.

III

I bursts the bonds of blood and bone
More often now as head grows bare –
Diving at dusk from a Greek cliff,
Heels rising over sea; sheets mussed,
Languorous beside a lover
For the first time; the House hushed
By a violin heralding
Violetta's death – being blanks,
Ego and *self* wink out, no sound, no
Clock ticks, no up, down, for a breath
All comes to view, math's phantom strings
Shivering beneath the stars beside
A loathed or longed for face,
Silver for sere indignities.

Will Eaves

I'm drawn to poems that try to consider contraries – the formal and experimental, the lyrical and the occasionally violent, the natural and the hallucinatory – without necessarily seeking their resolution or reconciliation. The themes are those of common experience: growing up, being in and out of love, enjoying the natural world both as a consoling and an alienating force. I write out of that experience and away from it; so that the end-product is true to, but unencumbered by, what has occasioned it. I don't really recognise the difference between intellect and feeling. In art, emotion is always mind-manacled.

The settings are various – the Australian bush, non-league football matches, gardens and highlands, charity shops – and probably reflect my sense that you can't ever *decide* to write about something; because writing, and especially poetry, is a sort of unforeseen targeting of life. The subject, whatever it may be, is captured without warning, like a view coming into sharp focus. What one might actually wish to be, as a writer, is of little account. You have to accept that – and it's liberating once you do.

From Weymouth

What made you wake me so early
And with a look of mischief say,
A start this fine's surely a sign
The sea is calling us today?
The train was blue, the water green:
A tinted postcard sent in May.

I'm sure I must have held your hand
In backstreets crammed with grockle shops
And pubs and reeling fishermen.
The smell I couldn't place was hops.
I rode in state along the beach,
Beside the ride that never stops.

I missed a few easy lessons.
The teacher smiled, as if to say
It's fine – it would have been a crime
To hear the call and disobey.
What did you do? The train was blue.
We had tea at a beach café

And well-thumbed fish-paste sandwiches –
That gritty complement to hours
Spent toeing desperately the line
Around two limpet-clad towers
The sea and I besieged, the moat
I'm sure I must have said was ours.

What made me want to go early
And with a look of mischief say,
But I'm hungry? You wrote in haste:
His Highness made the donkeys bray.
The train was blue, the water green.
Yours, waiting by the beach café.

Accommodation for Owls

The guest houses have shut for the winter.
The last bus out of here (and there are only two a day)
has gone. It's after five. And my new friends, Colin and Joy,
whose offer of a camp bed in an outhouse I've accepted gratefully,
are telling me about their courtship in the games room
of a mental hospital near Leith. *Axe-murderers.*

If I don't mind. Feel comfortable with the idea.
They fumble for a joke and go quiet.
We're sitting in a troglodyte's café-cum-shop
hewn from the rock – 'like Beethoven' – where
you can buy bacon and cream and bleached postcards
of green skies mantling Ben More, Mull.

The owner, moleish, fretful, spills sugar on the floor.
Aloud he says, though not to us, 'it can't be helped'
as if self-consciously remembering. Out in the bay,
his wife is winkling, spreading her salt-cured toes,
counting the grains that stick between
while others are dragged away.

Spare us your sympathy, Joy cries,
when over dinner I suggest 'it must have been awful'.
It was. A wilderness of frantic calm and Pictionary.
Nothing to read except Jumbo Puzzlers filled in and then crossed out.
Telly, of course. No radio. 'The things you missed were books.'
We walk down to the shore, clocked by Dervaig society:

A seal-like metronome
and high above the eagle's slow, unwinding beat.
Back at their stone-by-stone built house, Colin puts on *Kreuzer*
while Joy consults her concordance to Amerindian astrology.
I am an Owl with elements of the Goose. She yawns – it's almost one.
('Opinionated character. Night bird. Somewhat headstrong.')

Kickabout

I stopped sleeping and was afraid
that everything I did conveyed
the wrong message. A fat baldy allayed

my worst fears by ignoring them almost
completely. AFC Wimbledon, his club, could boast
Joe S., who once sat on the bench for Chelsea's first

team in the mid-'90s; and Darren D., reputedly
a mortician, who fired us three times past the post to deathless glory
in the Seagrave Haulage Counties League. We

went to every match, Baldy and me, our 57
obese with yellows and blues, him in his Saturday heaven,
me stupidly amazed to find that half of Raynes Park is Korean.

And it was therapeutic, I suppose,
to be a part-time bloke in borrowed clothes,
jeering the visitors from Basingstoke, cheering on those

especially who found an open goal and hoofed it wide.
I never wore the Dons' full kit, the colours. They implied
natural devotion, something unconsidered, more than pride:

comrades in arms, perhaps. Even the scarf I bought instead
felt too conspicuous. When I turned up, Baldy went red.
'I didn't recognise you like that,' he said.

Across Kingsmeadow's terraces a gale of tact
exposed the true self muffled when 'opposites attract',
my effort to be what another hadn't known he lacked

until he saw the lack forgiven by buffeted eyes.
We won the cup. We split up, to no one's surprise.
The house of sleep is full of spies.

Any Impediment

My love, there is a problem with the rats.
They're stuck together like chicken breasts.

If it were merely mingled tails and claws
I wouldn't mind, but some of them will

need a knife. What if the portions tear?
I do not want to see their bodies split

along a plane of tender grey weakness,
lest with the leakage and the residue

I should become appallingly familiar.
Upstairs your son's helical pet flickers,

catching the scent of strange deference,
the great taboo of what we find ourselves

doing mostly because we are afraid not to.
Forgive me, love. But I can't marry you.

Charity

Look at the posters in plastic frames,
Shirts boil-washed to fit a pygmy,
Ties from a school that was recently
Closed and turned into apartments.
All of a crime's precious evidence,
Here in the warm room of no claims.

Behind the till sits a codebreaker.
She was a young girl at Bletchley.
'Certain things stay in the memory
Whether or not they're important,
Often because they're not important,'
She says. 'It doesn't much matter.'

Look at the collars with real names,
Books, games, a stainless-steel trophy
Lifted, discarded, then bought by me
Knowing I wasn't the first or best
And that envy can be laid to rest,
Here in the warm room of no claims.

Three Flies

Three flies on a rock,
Orion's belt in negative,
a cold beer in my hand.
And, after the storm, the day's
hot handkerchief shakes out
a flock of butcher birds,
black holes for eyes, from
Sugarloaf and Mount Buggery.
Calicivirus thrived up here
and didn't stop at rabbits.
Cane toads shipped in to eat beetles
ate everything else instead.
That's pest control for you!
I smiled. Which maybe shows
I like a poisoned chalice – the
creek, the hut, the iced-bun
reek of sunblock and repellant.
Butchers wait in the trees all night.
The stars settle. It's pleasant.

Elegies Around Noon

1

I wish I could have sat with you more often,
downstairs, when you came in from the garden
and your afterlife of raising flowers
instead of kids: late roses, broom, hibiscus,
latterly a fig. The bramble by the steps
fruited for weeks, suckering closer
while I grew hopeful twigs, poked stones,
rolled words like 'forest' round my mind,
then heard you shout from the kitchen:
Christmas. Christ. Not again. I'd stained
the pastry red but everything was soon all right
and I was free to go back out while you stayed in.

2

You told us you'd been trapped in the pasture,
behind a strip of salt marsh and sea gorse,
by cows, advancing silent condemnation
of your drystone perch and deft picture.

'You have created a scandal
with your lunchtime desertion, Cecily,
leaving the herd to their ice cream-fuelled raillery;
to stubbed toes, sunburn, hit-the-can and tears, as usual.

They will miss you. They just don't know it yet.'
And frightened by such brown, eloquent eyes
in which the tide was high but turning,
you scrapped your drawing, and left.

A Year Later

Since you went back underground,
Into a world of solid waiting rooms,
Drip-fed arches and choked retreats,
You've been airily visible, present,
Returned, a burst seedcase and slow-
Growing regret: the morning light
Condensed where you once stood,
The dusky loss its own dividend.

Your sockets ogle worms' contrails
Crawling across the firmament, so
Near to voices you suspect of life
In a familiar house on a drained hill.
(To cloistered shades, sense-memory
Must tantalise the way the senses did.
What is this substitution for feeling?
Why can't I see the trampled sky?)

It needn't be that strange. You are
A dream – the self unself-aware –
And when a likeness raises you
(My rooky laugh, the waft of tea
Carried outside) we're not surprised
Though I have learnt to be discreet
And lower my eyes. To be recalled
You do not have to prove yourself.

Now all those duties become ours.
Your time of worry has given birth.
When most you're missed, I seem
To see a rope thrown ship to shore.
It has to flee the outstretched hand
And carve new purpose in the air.
Often the searching gaze conceals
The very thing it's looking for.

Evan Jones

Now, and maybe always, the poet's role as truth-teller, as conveyer of *aletheia* – meaning truth but literally 'not forgetting' (against Lethe) in Ancient Greek – has been downplayed to that of village idiot. The poet, one who does not forget, is an outsider, a misanthrope and a little digging into any poet's biography will only reinforce this stigma. But in the Ancient Greek, an *idiotis* was not necessarily a simpleton but someone who didn't take part in the affairs of the community – like a young man outside of a house who keeps tripping over his own feet trying to decide whether to go in and join the party (the literati) or just leave (go home) and who then does leave to write a poem about falling in love with a woman (literature, history, music, art) in a house while a woman (contemporary literature) who would fall in love with him waits in the kitchen (bathroom) of the house he just left, enjoying her drink (gin and tonic) but not the company (mostly novelists). Part of me is that young man, even now, searching for a way in without actually having to be there.

Little Notes On Painting

Take a Spanish painter and put him in Paris. Take a Greek
painter and put him in Madrid. Take a Quebeçois painter
and put him in Paris, too, and a German and a couple
more Spaniards and also a Greek-born Italian. You wouldn't
believe what I'm doing now. I'm up very late. I'm placing
an American painter in Albany and hoping school
will be cancelled tomorrow. There are fewer and fewer days
like this left; they fall like uses for wax paper. Don't ever
mention abstract artists to my face or my books, my friend, for
who owns a house and has never been kissed in one? Right?
Take a Russian painter and put him in New York beside
a Mexican painter. I am two feet from the bed; the pillows
and blankets are swelling and rising towards the ceiling.
It doesn't matter. Take a Javanese painter and put him
in Cairo. The phone won't ring anymore. I called a street artist
'Picasso' but thought better of it as all those women were
going down on him one at a time and bearing him children.
Take a little-known Nova Scotia folk painter and put her,
posthumously, in Cleveland or Skopjë. The mattress is filling
with honey and the box spring is humming like bees; my hand is
in my pyjama bottoms. I stop and say, it isn't love
that makes you weak, to the night table or maybe the bed frame.
Take an Italian Futurist for example. Take a nineteenth century
Japanese print and slip it between the mattress and the box spring.
Take a pregnant painter by the hand. I'm home and touching
the unborn child of her easel. It would be nice for a night
if silence was the colour of water but it would be nicer
to sleep in the desert. Take a stolen Brueghel from
the Kunsthistorisches Museum, Vienna, and bury it
on Easter Island. I arrange the sheets every morning
to resemble Mount Athos so that every night I sleep
on God's arm. What did I say about abstraction?
Take a British painter from a home he's not once ever loved
and ask him why he never paints the same thing. Take a moment
to join an art school, the aristocracy or merely buy
a beret. A photograph of a painter's palette is no good to
anyone and the sky outside is nothing like Van Gogh.
I just wanted to say that the moon's going down.
I remember every moment. Thank you.

Prayer to Saint Agatha

We can affirm nothing with confidence concerning her history... As an attribute in art her breasts, which were cut off, are often shown on a dish... she was credited with the power of arresting the eruptions of Mount Etna, so she is invoked against any outbreak of fire.

Butler's *Lives of the Saints*

Holy virgin of the third century,
martyr, refuter of married life,
pure thinker and resister of lechers,
I wished to write sooner, while you were young
and living among the countries of our
civilisation's birth. I have every
country in mind now and every childhood,
and you are a thousand women whose breasts
have been severed because of their beliefs.
I will say here something of life without you.

The kind of men you knew are gone. Women
are the same, though children may be too
serious, and we've spent most of the last
hundred years angry that our cries of 'Come
back to me,' to God and whoever,
go unanswered. No one falls asleep. Ships
sail over the desert and squirrels eat
from our hands. Taxis are yellow and films
end badly. Some of us try to hold on
to something, but there's no money in it.

I think of an apple. We have many
kinds now. Not one has given up its skin.
Not far from here, men garden and prune, trim
the lawn, and pink roses reach out to chew
the tyres off cars passing in the street.
Otherwise, we dine at the usual times
and sometimes even manage to speak
to each other. Meat and fish come frozen,
tomatoes don't taste like tomatoes, and
sandwiches are wrapped in paper and foil.

The ottoman is for feet, hair can be japanned,
noses roman. We will look the same
to you, perhaps taller, with our toes
knotted and fingers gnarled like rising
smoke. In May it rains. Sewers overflow
and spew out black tea, bits of wood, and lost
youths – the latter an army of millions
thought killed during the year's first snowfall.
On quiet mornings, you hear them calling
from the rivers running through the city.

And you, we lost track of you years ago.
Your skin must have hardened and dried, your bones
rotted through. There are images found in books,
hidden from air and outdoors; there are poems,
but not one of the words is your own.
A letter in a local magazine read,
'After reading this book I cried', and I
recognised you in it, though left unsigned.
And still today, as you rest your head on sleep's
shoulder, you must be the broad orange sun.

Martyr and holy virgin who shunned
the breath of living men in her ear, you are
a light shining through our dark sleep. I lay
my heart open to light. I wake at dawn
thinking of warm days and the sadness here
that will last forever. Nothing could be
forgotten. The people you never met
are growing older, they cannot change now.
I make this prayer to you on their behalf:
Please rid the world once and for all of fire.

Cavafy in Liverpool

Here is your sad young man:
he is ship-to-shore, he is buttoned-down
in tweed and scarved, eyes closed
when the Mersey wind

calls his collar to his ear
on the strand near Albert Dock,
some January, some winter day
we recognise but take no part in.

Here is your boy at the end of the shore
while the waters continue
touching place and nothing,
hold something dear and don't,

the desire and devotion
to an island he never dreams.
Not summoned, not answered,
he searches the world growing dim

as the river swells and recedes,
like closed eyelids shifting during sleep.
One less wave, he thinks, one less,
and then the Persians can get through.

God in Paris, 1945

Since the world ended He had been living
there, coming and going along the length
of the trembling Champs Élysées. Free
of the stars and prayer, His work tragically

out of fashion, the old city had seemed
as good a place to wander as any
and so, being wandering itself,
and swarming solitude, He paced along

the cobbled streets like a child lost in peat moss.
The Germans were gone, Céline with them,
and Jean Lumière singing *'Faisons Notre
Bonheur Nous-Mêmes'* in cafés stung His ears.

'Either the universe is infinite
or I am,' He remarked to passersby,
'Either the universe is finite or
I am. Or I'm not. Or I'd better be.'

If you reached out to touch His hand, even
accidently, you will remember Him.
For your hand is stone while your eyes and hair
are the wind that opens and shuts my book,

an ocean and sixty years away from
His room in the Hôtel du Marais, third
arrondissement, an unknowable land.
O rise wind, take my scattered pages

to vast and empty Paris. Either God lies
in a bed of earth alongside all
of history's dead or He doesn't. Or He'd
better. Whatever way wind, don't let up.

Bundesland Bavaria, Between Deffingen and Denzingen

Between Deffingen and Denzingen,
    summer opened the road
forward, browning the fields and hillsides
    of a country so barren
that the smallest horse grazing seemed
    resentful and withdrawn:
no longer seat-and-throne-of-men
    but pigeon-grey splotch
on the *Blaue Reiter* landscape, inured
    forever to the flow
of traffic, where once it drank from rivers,
    and aware of itself
as fodder for the glue factory,
    as much cattle as the cattle.
Between the route the Neckar runs
    and the dirty Danube,
neither the chatter of nits nor
    the bleatings of birds
on the horse's chest, its spreading ears
    folding over the wind
as night comes on. Then stones and woods
    stay no longer in their places,
begin to course, sing and wheel,
    like livestock once did,
leaving behind the parcel of the world
    over the larded breast
of Southern Germany: a resource,
    a wind through which
the horse rolls up to heaven
    its dull and stolid eyes.

Actaeon

Some names are words for grief,
graceless words for failure.
Actaeon was a crowd, a lonely man,
and in the end nothing,
awaiting his descent into simple witlessness,
cold beside a river of fire, who,
the story goes, either wandered
into a grove sacred to Artemis
and saw her bathing naked
or boasted he was the greater hunter.

And so, enduring the deep wrath of god,
thinking, No way out of this,
about to surrender it came to him that,
like any hound or creature in this world,
he too had yearned and hunted.

Later on in the underworld, he began to wonder
about symmetry, his cousin, unborn heirs
to the throne of Cadmus and whether or not
he'd been forgiven: a crowd, a lonely man,
nothing, awaiting his descent into witlessness,
and so cold near Phlegethon,
boundless river of fire.

Some men have grief in place of dreams.
How cold and sad an end those men will come to:
white caps over the blue, no linden trees
or red acorns under which to find shade,
and not one god to pray for mercy to.

Santorini

Certain days pass without a word between us,
where we walk in the street, always near the caldera
and she is younger than ever, pony girl, little donkey.

And in the nights following our days of walking
in silence, the world becomes shaped like a leaf
or a feather instead of always seeming so round.

The mornings that follow may be full of words
but these are unwelcome or maybe even unrecognisable
because so much has been said but not between us.

Our dream is to live here in this moment.
The road that begins near the museum curves up
as we walk, our feet becoming heavier, and 'Tell me',

one of us thinks, 'do you ever want some company,
or someone to make you dinner and breakfast?
So much time has passed in this way for others.'

Our dream is to live here in this moment, side by side
and walking in silence always along the caldera,
past busy cafés, expensive restaurants,

hotels, blue-domed churches, whitewashed houses and stores,
the light insisting along with the air that there
is no way to continue, to travel deeper.

But we find our way. The road winds past a store
selling postcards and if one of us thought,
'I could reach the sea from here', we would jump,

not because either is anxious to die but because
one would follow the other, prince or princess of lilies.
And to rise from the foam, clotheless, her skin all orange

and mine all brown – all eager to leave us behind –
and our eyes, peacock's eyes, filling with the sea
and salt and feathers. To live here in this moment

while trying not to repeat ourselves, walking
and looking down over the ocean, bodies built on top of bodies,
where all these things will be dust soon and are dust now.

When we reach the highest point we care to reach,
'Let's go', one of us thinks, 'we might walk down
not up this next time or else not bother jumping.'

Or we might at last take each other,
our dream of living in this moment over,
she in her short pants and I in my vestments,

the smell of pine trees everywhere.

Black Swallows from the Desert

after a Greek folk poem

My black swallows from within the desert
   and my white doves from somewhere on the coast,
should you fly anywhere near my home
   you'll see an apple tree in the frontyard;
if you land, could you tell my mother
   if she wants to become a nun, to retreat,
if she wants to dye her clothes black in mourning,
   she shouldn't wait any longer. Here in
Armenia, they've married me to
   a witch's daughter, an Armenian taken
to be my young wife, who casts spells
   over the skies and stars, casts spells over
fish and stops them swimming, casts spells
   over rivers and stops them flowing,
over the sea she casts spells and waves stop breaking,

she casts spells over boats so they stop sailing,
casts spells over me and I stop running.
   If I set out for home, snow and rain,
and when I turn back, sun and clear skies.
   I saddle my horse, it comes unsaddled,
I buckle my sword to my belt, it unfastens,
   I take paper to write but the sheet stays clean.

Henry King

Having grown up a Christian, and since apostatised, I often write poems into the spaces a vanished god leaves in the world. It is a world of specific places, in Britain and abroad, with their particular histories – just as words also have histories, which can impinge upon current meanings. Etymology may suggest complex connections, and make the literal metaphorical, the metaphorical literal: at moments of intensity, language and the body become indistinguishable, the word becoming flesh. In combining semantic richness with linguistic sensuousness, and in the sensible lineaments of form, poetry approaches incarnation – the guiding revelation in a world of uncertainty, where home is a hoped-for destination rather than a stable point of departure.

Adam

As she lay sleeping in the open air,
He lay beside her, listening for the sounds
That reached him faintly, coming from elsewhere:
Dogs calling in the dark, outside the grounds
He'd been confined to – somewhere out of bounds.

By day, their needs were all provided for:
They lived on fallen fruit and vegetables,
Talked, slept, had sex, and wanted nothing more
Until he heard, beyond the garden walls,
The baying, then the silence, of the wolves.

She woke not to 'good morning', but 'goodbye'.
They'd no possessions; all there was to pack
Was a rare fruit she'd brought for him to try.
He saved this to eat later, as a snack,
Then turned and left. He knew he'd not be back.

Theophany

No pillar today: low cloud supported
by spires and towerblocks
sags like the canvas roof of a tent
in a breeze that blows northwards but goes nowhere.

At night though, a column of smoke appears,
darker blackness blotting out stars.
Somewhere, a fire burns:
who keeps it alight? What fuel feeds it?

A man gets up at dawn every day,
takes out the ash and loads on more coal,
then reads a few verses, silently –
a ritual that's kept him warm, and his children.
But where are they being guided?

Over the city, the clouds break up slowly.

Vancouver

As the evening cools, we stand on the North Shore,
Watching the water, from Lonsdale to the sea,
And the sky above it harden to the same
Element: black and solid, lapidary.

Between them, over Downtown, a fissure
Has opened, where a molten sunset flows,
Too far away to warm us – till it sinks
Below ground, and the broken crust is closed.

If we were over at Point Grey, we'd see
The agitated lapping of the waves,
Like on the day we went there in a storm,
Discovering on that dirty beach the place

Was aptly named. Were we expecting peace
At the far end of the world? The revelation
Hidden by clouds and rain; only the water
Breaking and washing back, in constant motion...

But now car headlamps move across the bridges
In doubled lines, flickering in the dark
Like chains of fairy lights hung up for Christmas –
For which, these people are coming home from work;

And the roar coming up from the Inlet, day and night,
Is the wave that travelled North America
Breaking against the shore and washing back
Into the mountains, thick with pine and fir.

Sevenoaks

She takes me for a walk around Knole Park
To see the deer (though they've hidden beyond the trees)
And the great house, where only centuries
Before the last appear to have left a mark.

I've come here on a kind of pilgrimage
Late in Advent: crossing the narrow street
Through snow compacted by Donne and Sisson's feet,
I waded deeper into another age.

Before we leave the grounds by the west gate,
We hear the cars, and glimpse modernity
Written in vapour trails across the sky –
Even that's not a perfectly blank slate.

Lodgings and Belongings

A room composed of rectangles:
four cream walls, white ceiling, a window,
desk, bed, chest of drawers –
a box too bare and square for affections
to stick to. Now I'm going, they peel away
like blu-tacked posters, leaving hardly a smudge
to mark the twelve months it was mine.
It's as if I had never been.

Somewhere, there must be a room that still retains
a trace of me. But the one I grew up in
was long since emptied and refilled
with other people's lives: my bed with the scratched
wooden headboard, gone. Start again.

Tear down the pictures, pull books from the shelves,
torch the blinds and set the bed on fire,
because all the things that made each space a place
were things that happened there – or didn't, desire
cathecting even mass-produced furniture;
and the self that wanted what it now will never have
stayed locked behind those doors. Remember:
walk from room to room, listening to
your own breath, held in expectation so long.

No need to move, even: I already hear
my future footsteps echoing back to
this bare, square room, this box that's been mine a year,
and which I'll never leave.

To our Bodies Turn We Then

Suddenly awake in the early hours,
thirsty – dried out, perhaps, by the unaccustomed heat
of having someone in bed with me –
though half asleep, I'm half conscious
I'm not the person who lay down here.
Everything's metamorphic: the glass of water
is darkness made cold and hard; the body next to mine,
the same darkness become firm and warm;
we have no faces, and so long as we don't speak,
no names. We're no longer
our diurnal selves, with their ambitions and inhibitions,
who enjoyed polite conversation over dinner. We've become
those other ones: catholic and voracious,

not caring from whom we take our pleasure. Was it
to satisfy this appetite that we were driven
through all the preceding stages –
names, phone numbers, food, persuasion? If it was,
so our stranger selves could be released, and lie here
in the dark for a few hours, then who is this:
a prisoner or a prince? Ruler or ransomed?

                                   Later,
the monochrome light of dawn will enter the room,
restoring contours, and eventually, colour. We'll open
our eyes in mutual recognition, and only
the gentlest rapacity when we kiss betray
the person with whom each of us passed the night.

'It always points away…'

It always points away from earth.
Ascending into vacant air
Above this gothic church, a spire
Stands physically for the desire
To rise beyond the world, as breath

Indicates life. But though it crowns
The church, this sharply tapering
Spike has its root in suffering:
It emblemises how its king
Acceded to a wreath of thorns.

Fed by the plenitude of death,
It's natural that the brambles in
The graveyard should be overgrown;
Quickly passing it after rain,
It gives off a rich smell of earth.

Daphne

Might we, for a time,
be divested of our names?

By lamplight, we help each other
with buttons, clasps and zips,
letting our clothes drop
over the side of the bed, to fall in
an indiscriminate heap, leaving us
bare and shining. So,

might we just as easily
slip off these appellations
meant to mean who we are,
and just be – as a girl might step
from the tree in which she'd hidden?
Nobody gets that lucky;

but what was denied a god
a human may be given
out of grace: to hear your voice
unburdened of words, and watch
pleasure transfiguring your face.

Agnostic Epigrams

When asked what my religious viewpoint was,
I said I'm an agnostic – not because
            I think God may exist;
But, if He does, because He may be less
Angry to hear me say that than confess
            To being an atheist.

★

After I'd taken each side's deposition,
　　Compiled the facts, weighed up the evidence,
　　　　And looked at it from either point of view,

Then judged the most defensible position
　　Was where I was already – on the fence –
　　　　God was the first one I explained this to.

★

To slander God and question His existence
Like Baudelaire, with more or less persistence,

Springs from 'partial belief', as Eliot terms it:
Denying he has faith, one thus affirms it.

– Which partially explains the attraction blasphemy,
Despite its fallen shock value, still has for me.

A Windower

The house has too many rooms, now;
there's too much room in the bed.

A daughter in the Met, a son
at Cambridge; at home, long quiet spells.

On bright days, he stops by the window
looking into the garden. A windower.

Twenty, thirty years like this? Years
of evenings, weekends. Christmases.

Two Goodbyes

Down to the last things, now: the last
loaf of bread, pint of milk,
cups of tea.

Leaving, we keep the flat tidier
for strangers than we ever
did while living here.

The last things we'll have shared:
bread, milk,
little ironies.

★

A missed opportunity may still
exist; many are missed because
it seems they always will. And some
would do – but one stops taking them.

And so, I said 'I'll miss you', as if
you will still be near, and I'll
just fail to see you. No; not like that
at first. That is a later stage.

Voyeurs

Lying here, having woken up together
For the first time, our breath the only sound,
Our lips, not names, are on each other's lips.

Before last night, we fumbled with each other
In the obscurities of speech, until
We found ourselves in this lucidity:

Daylight falling through the curtains, tingeing
Your cheeks with a pink flush; your hair a halo,
Spread out across the pillow; your eyelashes

Glowing like filaments. But though I love
The candour of your skin, the tact with which
You leave so much unsaid, we can't escape:

Our words for lips, legs, fingers – the whole body –
Won't leave us be, but hover like voyeurs
Around the bed. We cower beneath the duvet.

I'd like to stay here for a little longer,
Simply to hold you and delay returning
To language one more hour. But when I do,

I find the words for every part of you
Have altered on my tongue: as if they now
Incorporate what they name, they've taken on

Your skin's warmth, taste and texture; and as such,
Enjoin, in conversations, the same silence
That we enjoyed there, needing nothing else.

I leave you, then, to go and waste my breath
In boring, bloodless talk, distracted by
The ordinary discourse of the day,

Till I find solitude to truly speak in:
Alone at last this evening, I'll be with you,
Lips slightly parted, savouring your name.

A Winter Evening

Trakl

Outside the house, the vesper bell
Tolls slowly; snow builds up in drifts.
The stores within are plentiful,
The table laid for many guests.

From far off, many wanderers come
Along dark paths to reach this door.
The tree of grace, now it's in bloom,
Draws moisture from the earth's cool floor.

A wanderer gently steps inside:
Pain turns the threshold into stone.
There on the board, by candlelight,
He finds a meal of bread and wine.

Rory Waterman

One can too easily say things that don't really stand up even to one's own scrutiny; what follows should be understood as tentative.

The poem I initially want to write is not necessarily the poem I end up with, and sometimes the two are distant cousins. In other words, the process of writing is often also one of finding out: as E.M. Forster said, 'How can I tell what I think till I see what I say?' A few of these poems, such as 'Driftwood' and 'Family Business', came in their entirety in one go, but most take a lot longer and use up several trees in the process. All seem to begin with a desire to communicate something when the fog in my head clears, an experience rare enough to ensure that when it happens I do what I can to drop everything: 'Nettles' was drafted on the back of a receipt on a windy May evening, when I was knee-deep in a nettle patch in Lincolnshire with a carrier bag and a pair of kitchen scissors. At the heart of some are intensely autobiographical experiences, but I do very much hope to connect with other people on *their* terms. Few things are more gratifying.

For my friend Richard,
with thanks and admiration.

Hawthornden Castle
19/i/2012

Out to the Fen

Suddenly, the shattered hedges, ancient culverts,
our huge ruined villages, give way as
dimpled fields tilt to the Fen
and the treeless otherworld begins.

A farmer churns a vast parched field to a desert of stalks
in acres of dust and haze. Blueflies thrum
unperturbed, by a verdant ditch straight
as a Midwestern state highway, vanishing both ways

into hardly a ridge: a slope that stretches
and loops for hundreds of miles to the same sea.
Along its lip, behind dykes, the low farms and
hardened cottages stare across the flats.

It's like a coast, but what might be sea
is a sea of outstretched meadows, fresh green wheat
nodding like so many donkeys,
dotted with clumps of poppies,

and the elders have flowered. We snip
the heads by dusk, in a silence of ditch noise
and birdsong, for cordial and fritters,
sometime later, then scatter

hares in the headlamps, and thud through clouds
of skitting gnats as distant lights
blink to let us know buildings are
over there, people are over there, and now

it's time to go.

Family Business

The boatman stares through million-pock-marked waters,
tapping a cigarette, shying from the rain
in mac and wellies, beneath a London plane
that rustles and drips. He turns and tells his daughter
to bolt the hut. Tonight the summer's over.
He heaves the skiff to the boatshed, ties the lines
and double-locks the door. She fits a sign:
CLOSED FOR SEESON. They load a battered Land Rover
with cash tin, radio, stools, as fast as they can,
for it's raining harder. Lightning blanks the dark,
and then they're away, the wiper thwacking its arc.
She glances at this ordinary man
then shuts her eyes: she's damp and tired and bored.
He drives more gently. Neither says a word.

Nettles

I go to harvest nettles in the wood
with vaguest thoughts of soups and stews and teas,
and wade through stems that break

across my knees, not thinking of the wreck
my steps have made, remembering my Nan
using an afternoon to gouge and twist
her shadow with a spade

for rhubarb that we never ate,
for jams we never made.

What Passing Bells

A policeman blocks the road so I stop
and tut and tap the wheel and find a sweet
and scrape it through its wrapper with my teeth.
More cars stop. Then bright rustling up the street
from snare drums and some reedy trumpet calls
remind us all what day it is. In front

the noise grows to a wail. The band files past,
the soldiers, local groups, then ranks of kids
half out of time, with backs and shoulders stiff,
some looking at us looking at them for
just long enough to say a thousand words
in glares. They don't remember any wars

but TV ones, and nor (confess) do you:
just TV wars, most justice-compromised
in barren lands, for rich commodities
I'm using up, a quiet friend by my side
with best intentions, clothes from Oxfam shops,
our flask packed for a cold stroll by the sea.

The Lake

Mid-May now, and the hawthorns have started
foaming and stinking. They glow under clear night sky.
The car park is empty, the vending hatches shut.
When I was too small to stand somebody left
a girl near here to die, unconscious, full of come,
and gagged, in case. Flopped her in the silt
with care. The moon flutters a meaningless smile
and on the surface it skits everywhere.

Growing Pains

1 DISTANCE

Mummy goes to court and Daddy goes
to court, poppet, and in there they sort out
what happens next, love – where you go to bed
and go to school. That's all this is about.

And who deserves you most? Who's the best
at cuddling you and saying never mind
each time you piss the bed? It's like a test
and you're the prize, my sweet. The experts know,

they've done their sums and read their clever books.
That judge man, he's a clever clever man.
So be a big boy, kid, and dry your eyes.
We all love you. We're doing all we can.

And now – my word! – you're twenty-five years older,
pulling affidavits from a folder.

2 FOR MY FATHER

...discord which has ripped
you from your father, stripped
away known places, play and friends...

Andrew Waterman, 'For My Son'

So I grew up a 'case', in Lincolnshire,
'abducted', as you'd have it, just turned two,
when 'she revoked [my] birthright'/ brought me here.
This is my tale of 'access times' with you:

Daddy came each month. On Saturday
the social worker's car would take me down
to the Lindum Guesthouse, seven miles away
in Lincoln, then we'd hug and walk around

the shops, and up the hill to Castle Square –
a gape-mouthed gatehouse one way, and the other
the honeyed Minster penetrating air.
And, in another world, my loving mother.

For this was Daddy's place. You taught me how
the Normans built those arches, how that well
gave Romans all their water from the brow
of this glacial hill, beneath which Celts

came sliding in small boats to Brayford Pool,
where Vikings later came to overhaul
and settled with the natives. At my school
we hadn't 'done' this yet, us boys and girls

all learning to fit in, and here I stood
in my home town and breaking it apart
with Irish Daddy, near to whom I slept.
Then Sunday would arrive and I'd depart

full of stories, tears, cake, love, resentment,
our candle burning brightly to a stub
in Lincoln Minster, seven miles away,
as I got home and you got to the pub.

A swift one for your long hard journey home.
And though I didn't love one of you more
the cries and bedtime hugs with Mum at home
were urgent, but it's you whom I cried *for*.

And that was most of it. Remember how
I'd speak into the Dictaphone? 'Explain'
my feelings on where I'd 'like to live now',
in a town I'd only heard of, called Coleraine,

whilst sitting in the Lindum, downing sweets?
At two I'd not grown used to anywhere.
By five the squat stone houses, leafy streets
of Dunston, rural Lincolnshire was where

my life was, if for better or for worse.
The court heard our recording and agreed.
And Lincoln was a blessing and a curse,
where Daddy lived each month, and lived with me.

3   IRELAND, 10

'This is your homeland.' Looking at
a row of mountains for the first
time in living memory –
that child of sunken Lincolnshire,
      of flattened vowels and reticence –
      I knew that it was not. And why
      he wanted it to be.

Those Ireland shirts he'd put me in
on access visits! Toddling round
a chipped bust of King George III
in Lincoln Castle, sporting green,
      had fractured me. The first house that
      I'd known, where he still lived, and drank,
      no more to me than photographs

until that week. But always my
'other home'. The leafy bank
I'd dreamed was there, behind that lens,
thick and wild with gooseberries
      and blackberries, rosehips and thorns,
      like mum had, was a breezeblock school
      for Catholic kids with uniforms

and habits that I didn't know,
accents, odd names, ginger hair,
school holidays at funny times.
I'd watch them through the window, there.
      Then back at school and flooded with
      a slurry of ineptitudes
      I'd brag about that 'other home'

and 'other me' – not *here*, like *them* –
the Irish me that never was,
the bronze-haired friends I never made,
the mansion where dad never lived.
            And mourned the loss of all these things
            I'd never had and always had;
            and grew, estranged from Lincolnshire
            and desperate to get out of there.

Driftwood

Found, gathered, arranged in sizes, lit.
We huddle in their element, watch sparks
explode from ancient wood, embroider soot.

Those packs of soup decanted into pots
bubble to licking flames. We can't catch fish.
We're playing games, as close now as we dare
to what our forebears, as we think them, were.

53.093336°N latitude / 0.253420°W longitude:
07/2010 capture: street view

I remember, I remember
How my childhood fleeted by, –
The mirth of its December
And the warmth of its July

Winthrop Mackworth Praed,
'I Remember, I Remember'

A lodge house to an estate, once: the front wall
still ends with one redundant brick gatepost,
its rustic latch clicking only to wind,
and the clean bulk of its limestone cap
shorn of clogs of English ivy, carious and precarious.

There used to be a long metal water butt
out of bounds, snug to a wall, pungent
with moss and webs, its content a black
lilting mirror when I'd raise the lid
that was wooden and rotten and gave slightly.

And there was a low-slung roof on a breezeblock annexe
with a fat windowsill and convenient external piping
that occasionally broke and had to be mended;
and a cigar box of old green pennies and shards of pot
from the garden, out of sight in a cracked soffit.

But the side gate remains, a wrought iron cross-hatch
mass-produced in a distant foundry, showing
bends for the feet that are no longer mine,
that kicked off and made it a shrill, dull swing;
and the fence is the matt-green my grandmother painted,
but tarnished now, and in places peeling.

Winter Morning, Connecticut

Your parents' house. Your bedroom full of books
and photo albums. Clothes you won't throw out.
The Hepburn calendar, a decade old,
silted, faded, skewered to a wall.
The bed you might have shared with other men
when they were boys, the bed that went with you
to university.

We leave it, drink hot coffee, bundle up
and step out on a lawn of blazing snow,
shedding lines of prints that drift apart
and back together, let our stumbles show
and find us huddled here
with soft bright pellets scattered through our hair
as though embroidered there.

A Suicide

Away. And for a moment as you tipped,
traversed the awful point of no return
and yelled, stretch-torsoed in the faraway,

you faced us. Eyes unseeing mirrored mine:
I thought of me; the you in me, in us;
and all the things you'd given us to say.

Back in the Village

Where did that child go, straying down the lanes
in thinning snow, seeing footsteps turn
to slush then rain, one cold, eventless day;

or clambering through the ruined manor house,
all done up now, worn-in and trellis-guarded?
He knows their cellars and lofts better than they
do still, I'm sure. Where is that child today?

He's outside what was Paul's house, with his wife,
in silent night beneath crisp constellations –
star-swarms and nests of secret nebulae –
the car on gravel by the village pub.
He's walking round The Green, where once he played

throwball – that's a game his mates invented,
dependent on a tree that's been removed.
New children wouldn't know that one had stood there
and wouldn't give a tuppence anyway.

He's leaning on the sign by his old school:
new roof, new teaching staff, much else the same;
kids home asleep (tomorrow is a school day).

He's nothing to them; all of this is theirs.
He's handed down the torch, though, in a way.

Keepsakes

Chairs and *chaise longues* arranged for sitting in,
with teasels in their hollows; china cups
on gate-leg tables, with tortoiseshell snuff boxes,
Bakelite telephones and Toby jugs,
some chipped with web-cracked noses; dull mirrors that warp
the roomful as I pass them, or fatten my legs;
a photo of a soldier from the War,
oak-framed, mouthing something, buttons white
with sun-fading and Brasso, marked as 'Scuffed';
the constellation of brass companion sets
taking up a corner at the back;
the bawdy cards and hunting prints and pastels
marked 'LINCOLN MINSTER', and flocks of shimmering Spitfires
whirring up through bold faux-Whistler skies
in stark formations, on to Victory
in masses of blues and whites and tangerines.

More pictures than wall, more bric-a-brac than floor.
A century and some of neglect, of cleared-out houses,
of looked-after-then-left. Old trades and whims
offered up in clusters round a hall,
away from wet and rot, not allowed to be junk,
whatever once they meant. Vague familial
discarded worlds that died and hide in us.
And that is what my mother comes here for.
So now we're back in Horncastle again,
for a day under buzzing strip-lights in cold rooms
and frogmarching a cabinet to the car,
a Victorian planter, Edwardian wine tables,
for her to look at sometimes, bring out for guests;
long hours of agreeing things are nice,
half-bored, slow-stepping round tat.
But cherishing it, a little bit, perhaps.

Sheri Benning

We hold inside of us a constellation of the places we have previously inhabited; our sense of self grows out of and reflects our home-places. Ethnographer Keith Basso writes that when places are actively sensed, the physical landscape becomes wedded to the landscape of the mind. In keeping, my writing practice is galvanised by my experience of growing up on a small farm in Saskatchewan, and, in pace with my peripatetic lifestyle, the experience of always leaving.

Places acquire deep meaning through daily, almost nameless intimacies, which often pass unnoticed; however, art can illumine these fleeting moments of care. With poetry, I attempt to excavate layers of dwelling, to lend sensible form to the inconspicuous moods and rhythms of home.

Refashioned from the remnants of the family farm, I hope my poems are a kind of reliquary that stands in the wake of our high-speed pursuit of global capital. We continually lose our places to ecological devastation. By rendering visible the unthought potencies that engender home, I hope my poetry quietly asks: if we constantly abandon our places, do we lose connection to what sustains us?

Dusk

Hyacinth petals, wet, on cobblestone. Late afternoon. Smell of burning oil.
Rain pitching a tent of night, I thought of you.

After the parade, streamers and beads strewn down the close. In a doorway
a man smokes a cigar. The echo of drums turned my heart into a bruise; at
the back of my throat, the taste of burning oil.

Remember that hungry-eyed child, her mother barefoot, who watched as
we waited for the train in Moscow? Our love so decadent, a mouthful of
meat, my stomach turned when she begged for food in the stations' stench
of burning oil.

Now Edinburgh's tenements, darkened by coal smoke, remind me of you
– how you came home to our flat with black bread and fruit, the candle-
light through our kitchen window glowed at dusk like burning oil.

By the position of its stars, the Elsheimer painting can be dated 1609, late
June. I'm stunned by a longing so precise, by a lake lit by moon, its sheen
the colour of burning oil.

Silence

The moment stands still… space is filled with a dense silence which is not absence;
it is the secret word, the word of Love, who holds us from the beginning.
                                        Simone Weil. *Seventy Letters*

You asked me what kind of silence is moon
silence and I'm standing at my kitchen window watching
August moon gather into its apron wings
of mist from the lake.

Ringed in dusk incense –
pine, balsam, reed grass, cricket hum –
the moon is a henna-stained palm, cupped.
I haven't answered your question, though. Remember

when you asked me if I could name my pain, find it in my body?
You said yours was in the marsh of your chest, a red-winged
black bird nesting in prairie sedge. I believe inside of me,

behind the oak doors of hips, there is a dim room with a table.
A broken loaf of bread, a wine-stained glass. Someone was there
and left. Light from a candle shoots spasms
through the cave of me.

But this room isn't really empty, is it?
It's full of the silence you've been trying to show me
with your questions. Red-henna moon rising over lake.
Brief flare of wings over cattails. An empty glass. Surfeit

silence that is not loss, but something that offers
to be held. Not absence, but a hushed
word of love.

Vigil

to Sarah

I am no longer young. I know what we love,
we will lose. Your head resting in my lap
as you hold your newborn to your open breasts,
milk scent, mown hay. Snow falls

beneath the street lamp's glow,
flutter of her eyelashes as you nurse her into dreams
of light and shadow. I read in the tow of candles
we lit to mark this evening's coming.

With my free hand I gloss dark waves of your hair.
All I want is to unknot what anchors you here,
to ease you into sleep. If I could read the notes
of your new mother's heartbeat

that I feel against my thighs,
they'd be a lullaby –
>   *Don't be afraid. We love*
what we will lose. I am not young anymore.
Your body sighs, you slip
into sleep's undertow,
the anchor rope,
tossed to shore.

Plainsong

Driving home from Uncle Richard's,
                    in the backseat with my brother and sister –
weft of limbs, pearlesence of moonlit skin,
                    shift and fall of their breath.

My face against the car window to watch stars, and every mile
                    a farm, yard-lights,
a voice in plainsong –

                    after feeding the cattle, Dave Saretsky stepping into his porch,
                    borscht warming on the stove,
                                        hambone, pepper, cloves.
      She's tucking in their youngest boy,
                    her palm on his feverish cheek.
      After, she and Dave will sleep, in the space their bodies have learned
                    to make from years of sharing
                                        blood, spit, loam –

Blink of frost on wheat stalks, fields left in stubble to snare
                    October's first snow-squall, the tip of dad's cigarette
      knots of smoke, mother singing lowly to the radio,
                    the gypsie-light of stars and farms,
                                        a raw harmony

like the dark wave of geese lifting off the slough just east of our barns.
Their winter homing, a folksong for the journey
to where flesh might belong.

Our farm's sold. Dave's too. Uncle Richard died seventeen years ago,
and only now the light of this memory reaches me; its source, gone.

Listen

Fall. The season of listening for what we must let go. But your listening was something hungry, a demand to be spoken to. To be heard. Now far from him you remember two things. Probably accidents or undeserved gifts. Like the slant way you realize spring – weak-tea light of dusk, wrist's moon-shadow when you hold the hot cup. A knowing that slinks through your gaze. But you're doing it again. Please. Just listen.

Driving with him to work. Morning moon passing through pine – sleight of hand, shocks of silver. The story of the farrowing sow. How as a kid he sat in the broth of straw, burnt wood, manure. Furious mewing, steaming birth, he'd place the litter in a box of rags, cut their teeth, return them to their mother. How he and his brothers took turns waiting. Head wrapped in scarves of sleep, he'd break the night-mirror, split light of snow-stars pooled in alloy sky. How he sang stories to stay awake.

You realise you are panicking. You want to free him from the scars of smoke, work, whiskey, that tear him from the small songs he made in front of the fire where he learned how to wait.

Listening has made your heart a bruise, a dark pearl of gravity. Outside your cabin, the great blue heron rising each morning, a gesture of abandonment to what is more. It shames you. You watch the moon finally sink into a barbed crown of unlit pine and not rise. That's the only thing you can recall with any sort of clarity – the moon's last time and with such voiceless ease.

That song that goes

For no reason I can name
I look away from the book and see
the moon deepen into golds and reds.
Eastern sky a sodden blue. Spring
dusk is something to breathe deeply --
wet dirt, stubble, last year's leaves.
And like a dream that comes back
only when unasked for, I recall
his hands from when I was a child –
rough wood, tobacco, metal of earth.
A friend tells me of early grey mornings
at his kitchen table. There was tea,
the beginnings of a wood-fire, his wife,
bread. And the winter river bed, the long,
slow ache I carry inside, briefly fills
with the singing of spring melt.
Memory is that song the heart hums
along with. The one without
thinking, beneath breath.

Near the river

Three years later, you see her. The child who called *Mama!*
every day, late afternoon. Her voice rose in the courtyard

beneath your bedroom window – first snow, pigeon down, wet newsprint,
and the oil stain of night seeping over the embankment of the Neva. *Mama!*

and you look up from where you sit now, near the Saskatchewan river,
its hills like the flanks of running horses. Grasses pared

by summer's last heat. Between your fingers
you roll chokecherries, blood-shot pouches of skin

beneath tired eyes. The dusk moon, exhaled breath
of a whitetail, is snagged on aspens, *Mama!* and you watch

her run down the steps, two at a time, into her mother's arms.
You feel her small body, the warm heave of her chest

as she leans into her mother's thighs like that moth-flutter
of pulse you once held inside. *Mama!* Chokecherry pulp

has stained your fingers red, and as you walk away,
the moon in the aspens loosens and lets go.

Fidelity

At last the fidelity of things opens our eyes

Zbigniew Herbert

Once my sister was sick. So much had happened to her body
over which she had no say; it lay dormant in her sinew for years.

But then, the aftershock –

I sat beside her when they slipped her body into the MRI.
I wanted to hold her, but couldn't, so I prayed

as though I was a bargain-hunting pauper willing to trade up
glass beads and feathers, something as useless as my life,

for her safety. As though a prayer could be anything
other than a plover's nest in marram grass, vulnerable

to what is always devastatingly unknown.
That night driving in Saskatoon, she didn't believe

the moon could look like it did, so I drove her to the edge of the city's halo.
Hemmed in by wheat and barley, glow of a bare bulb in the root-cellar

of August dusk, we hung our heads out the car windows
into cricket hum. Stars and there it was –

moon, a cupped palm, sallow,
and ready to receive.

Vincenz Serrano

In my work, I place discrepant things side by side. Placement is bound to displacement: materials come from sources, things have origins, quotations come from voices, names have etymologies, stories come from lives, forms have histories. Juxtaposition takes elements from old contexts and embeds them in a new milieu, a disorientating act that offers new ways of thinking and feeling. Drawing from the work of Nick Joaquin, Eric Gamalinda and Gina Apostol, who employ innovative aesthetic techniques to represent Philippine history in their poems and novels, I use parataxis – in references, language registers, images, and genres – as a way of remembering, using methods akin to rearrangement. A refusal of past fixities is a refusal of present and future foreclosures. At the same time, it is an opening up to possibilities. This, for me, is where poetry becomes inseparable from history.

Cornerhouse

A couple is waiting for their meal. There's a drawing on the wall nearby. A family of six rides a motorcycle. Three children on the curb watch them pass. There's graffiti behind the children: the Statue of Liberty, but instead of a face – eye sockets, a hole not a nose, teeth. The man reads a magazine. The woman reads a book. The meal arrives: sandwich, soup. In my city, often, families ride motorcycles too, even on highways, where buses speed past. In provinces, to accommodate more, the motorcycle driver adds planks. The driver has difficulty balancing. Still, everyone moves forward, as wobbly as a country with too many children and not enough books, too many breaths and not enough meals. The man looks at his sandwich; he looks at her; he nods. The woman looks at her soup; she looks at him; she nods. On a seat next to the couple are magazine and book. Stasis is balance in disguise; it is wobble holding its breath: woman, teeth, sandwich, eyesocket, motorcycle, country, man, soup, book, chair, magazine, children, table, curb, face. One moves. The other withdraws. Someone shifts. A motorcycle tilts. The curious gather and watch.

If you can't see my mirrors I can't see you

– sign on van

We walk apart along various streets, lost from each other's view, then see each other again elsewhere, perhaps courtyard, perhaps alley. Pedestrians, push-carts, jeepneys, poles, wires, tricycles, and vendors clutter the scene. If we shift our lines of sight, we would, obliquely and fleetingly, be visible to each other. For instance, if you buy bottled water in a shop, I would see you, on a mirror where ceiling meets wall, take change from your pocket. Perhaps on a window of a barbershop, you can see my reflection. But the city is ruth-lessly solid: a shoe left on the street, telephone poles on which one finds phone numbers of plumbers, façades of buildings whose paint has half-peeled. An origin of the word *mirror: speculum* – reflective surface – from which is derived – *speculate*. Along R. Hidalgo are houses of the turn-of-the-century well-to-do. From these houses in the city center used to come piano music, sound of sculptors' hammers and chisels, smell of smoked meats and caramelised sugar, hushed prayers at dusk, sound of capiz windows opening then closing. Now houses are taken over by the poor. Scholars say that after the Second World War, the rich went elsewhere in the city, the poor settled in spaces that once smelled of tobacco smoke and fabrics made of fine pineapple fibers, tramlines that the war destroyed were never rebuilt and so came jeepneys. This is how a scholar speculates: he finds facts as solid as things – aluminum, tin, glass – and changes them into possibilities as miraculous as mirrors. Some, though, would no longer call this scholarship but artifice. From an overpass on Quezon Boulevard, I see you walking along stalls of pirated DVDs, bicycle shops, videoke bars, vendors of underwear, vendors of knives. Facts can be gathered the way a mirror gathers detail or a place gathers noise, silence, floodwater, shadows. Mirror also comes from *mirer* – to look – from which is derived – *mirage* and *miracle*. You once asked me: where is the moistness in your poem. It was like asking: where in your city is its history. Moistness is something discerned from an angle. Tell all history but tell it slant. We are again lost from each other's view but once in a dark room I saw two films projected at right angles to each other. The images screened were that of two filmmakers filming each other as they walked in opposing directions. Even though they walked in spirals – one inward the other outward – they kept their cameras focused on each other, keeping each other in view even as they were moving away. Telephone wires are entangled with electric wires, alleys with boulevards, cul-de-sacs with streets, pedestrians with prayers, miracle with mirage, poor with war, I with you. With entanglement comes moistness. One sculptor, unlike others, did not leave. He continued making statues of religious figures for processions, churches, houses. The Black Nazarene statue at Quiapo Church had fallen into disrepair, the parish priest asked the sculptor to make a replica. Each year, in January, from noon to night, the statue would go around the streets of Quiapo in the midst of crowds. Crowds wanted to catch a glimpse of the suffering Christ. People would throw cloth, handkerchiefs, towels, and shirts at the statue's attendants, who would wipe these on Christ's face then throw them back. To attend a procession is to fulfill a vow. To vow is to be entangled with God, from an angle, amidst the smells of crumpled towels and sweaty shirts. When the new statue was done, the sculptor and parish priest paired the old body with the new head, new body with old head, we do not know on which version our sorrow is wiped, to which version we pray, videoke music becomes louder at dusk, jeepneys move on the ghosts of tramline routes, we speculate, spiral, the city stands at a tilt and an angle, a camera is a crowd of mirrors placed at an angle, after which come moistness, replica, mirage.

Short Walks

To walk through a city is to cut it into parts: like a wound or a landscape the city opens, then like a scab or a room it closes. My scholar and I move in a pace so slow it is like postponement. When we walk through a city we hurt it, my scholar says: we make it aware of how much it is against itself. Our shadows are the bruises of buildings, our slowness keeps the wound from healing, our being together means we are prone to surprise: this church, clouds, that house, chance, this sweat, glance, that touch.

Show your face, dear city, then hide, says my scholar. How you reveal yourself is inseparable from how you conceal: it is a gesture called history. My scholar loves a street that leads to a point along a riverbank, ends where another street begins, ages along with its buildings, becomes blind corner, betrays its old name for a new one. In the ache of opposites, the city knows it is alive: crowd and solitude, old and new, beauty and decay, feeling and fact, silence and noise, grasp and emptiness. Make sense of this with me, says my scholar: if we talk to the city, how the city responds is a clue to how we shall be together.

I disagreed with my scholar's way of thinking. I wanted to take things apart. In the city there is a steel church whose parts were made in another country and then sent here on separate ships. I thought to do the opposite: pry things apart, set the parts adrift, observe how dismantlement leads to the new: a dialogue between buttress and transept, nave and steeple. The streets which my scholar loved made sense to me, but only after going through a method akin to derangement: arriving at the unknown after a long period of poison, suffering, disorder. Melt the steel of the steeple and create money. Take in water from the river and make thirst. Put two people side by side and produce silence.

My scholar believed that separate things, even if they were in pain, comprised a whole; I believed that the distance between particulars, the space between statues and plazas, the blank between noise and sublimity, a gap between a river and the knowledge of itself, had to be maintained by force: the parts would cohere only when they could overcome the force that kept them separate. But this would entail so much violence that when the parts merged they would no longer be recognisable. In other words: ugliness. In other words: the new.

On the day we parted, my scholar said: in another time, walking was slow incision, people walked led by tortoises. Umbrellas, boots, liquor, curl of shopkeeper's moustache, history of objects on display: the slowness made shapes and sounds and stories clear. I cannot describe my talent for causing a swiftly-ruined thing, but for penance I took walks, without tortoises but pilgrim-slow: hence these words that follow, hence silences, hence the blanks that link you and me, hence crowds, hence clues, hence a kind of motion that opens shut things, as when one is in a room collapsing into the size of departure, one sees bodies approaching each other – which one is me, which one is you – like lips of a wound that never close into a kiss.

R. Hidalgo

Cliché to say crowds reside in a loner cliché to say in you
there are multitudes cliché to say a crowd is an image of loneliness look
at that woman going down the underpass who will she be once
she emerges on the other side like an aphorism about to fall in love
with gossip.

Anloague

For years he built houses made of wood and thatch and when stone and tile became fashionable he swam down the river and was never seen again.

Quiapo

There are two statues. The head of the first
is true. Its torso and limbs are copies. The torso
and limbs of the second are true. Its head
is a copy. If I tell you which one goes out every year
to be touched by crowds you would see
how much of you inhabits me. Truth copy
limb crowd twin touch copy torso.

Bilibid Viejo

Hands tied, eyes blindfolded, feet bound.
Passersby talk about where they had gone.
Listening is the only way you can travel from now on.

Estero Cegado

I was open.
        In consequence, moments were taken from me without my knowing.
I was unkind.

Nevertheless, desire looked at me from head to foot.
I was occupied.

In the meantime, from inside buildings voices spoke into mirrors.
I did not know how to love without ruining the other.

In another city, shadows teach
light how to shine by refusing to cast themselves on surfaces. In the absence
of shadows light burns more brightly, out of horror.

Hormiga

Perhaps smallness perhaps longing perhaps the linking
of streets perhaps laughter perhaps satiation perhaps
a way of entering another wherein compassion was
indistinguishable from violence perhaps pausing
perhaps a glance perhaps breathing perhaps another.

Ongpin

A walk is a form of tenderness not slow enough to mean *let's be st'll*, not
fast enough to mean *let's flee*.

San Sebastian

There was little time left before parting.

We stayed there the longest.
It has withstood war and earthquake for it knows how it began:
in pieces, complete only in the mind, then in fragments coming in –
pillar, steeple,
buttress, altar – parts of a lack longing for the opposite of upheaval,
one by one arriving from far away.

Static

When songs,

> He stuns flies; fluid oozes from their abdomens. He places flies on the

advertisements,

> ground and waits for ants. Some flies recover and escape; most do not.

and programs

> With their mandibles, ants grab flies' legs and inject venom into their

end, I begin.

> bodies. Some flies flail, but stop resisting when the venom takes effect.

Resemblance

> The ants take the flies back to their colony. He wants to see where they go

to wash and

> but they pass through cracks in the wall. The ants left behind encircle the

hiss of sea. I

> remnants of the fluid. He does this during late afternoons in childhood; in

flow into places

> the film, he is working on a teleportation system. The system is comprised

parched in silence:

> of two telepods connected to cables and a computer. The system can

shoe racks, compost

> teleport an object but not a living thing. The computer program breaks it

pits, door

> down into atoms, transmits then reconstructs it. The computer does not yet

hinges, spaces

> know what flesh is. Flesh breaks down but cannot be put together: what

between raindrops,

> enters as dog emerges as tissue, fluids, bone, whimpers. It is only after he

the interval

> falls in love that he understands flesh. He reprograms the computer. He

between thirst and

> teleports a baboon. He then wants to teleport a human – himself. He goes

water. Unlike

> inside one telepod, the door closes, sparks fly, the other door opens, smoke

a wave I neither

> comes out and so does he. However, he does not know that a fly is in the

arrive nor depart, it

> telepod with him. The computer, instead of putting them together

is the water that

> separately, fuses them. He knows something only in terms of another. To

moves, not

refer to points in a map is to disclose parts of the self. What has happened

the sea. I have

to one's body gives another a glimpse of a city's history. When he was a

no tempo no

guerilla during the Second World War, he was, it was said, impervious to

tone no melody

bullets. He had taken an amulet which supposedly had the power to make

no lyrics yet I

bullets miss their mark. He would run between buildings, hide behind

inhabit hearing

trees, and after encounters, his comrades would find bullets lodged in bark

the way faint

and brick, but not in his flesh. In the telepod, man and fly merge; in the

lights haunt

body, an amulet is lodged within tissue, fluids, bone; in a paragraph,

the eyes, or how

elements enter, flail, resist, become embedded to each other and then

a farewell

break away, it is the speech among elements that makes the silences of the

lingers in the

design. A few days before he dies, he coughs up a small rough black

station after lovers

object. She prepares herself for his death: that's it, she says, he's near the

board separate

end. Medals, citations, and wedding photographs are on a wall, what

trains. I am

enters as stone emerges as amulet, there are places where the paragraph

the sound

turns to break, he who stuns flies is the I who writes in disguise, man

of cliffs

becomes fly, without the amulet he dies. He at first does not die, but he

crumbling at

does not remain human. As days pass, parts fall off – nails, teeth, nose –

the embrace

and other parts change: hair becomes tough as wire, saliva as corrosive as

of waves. I

acid. He crawls on walls and the ceiling. He breaks his dinner down with

am in the straits

saliva, sucks the fluid, vomits it, then sucks it back in. He tells his lover –

of night's

I'll hurt you if you stay – so she leaves, but not for long, he who becomes

bandwidth,
        fly stuns his lover undisguised, we move towards each other and corrode
between the
        into closeness. It is not yet night, it is no longer love, I am not yet me, we
trough and
        are no longer in each other's mornings, not yet in each other's moments,
crest of my
        it is the instant that moves and not time. The body is made up of decay. A
voice until
        poem is assembled out of voices taken from various mouths. A moment
morning takes
        carries another moment in its mandibles. The future is the present passing
away the ocean
        through cracks in the wall. On the other side, let me merge with who I am,
of my speech.
        and come out undisguised.

Janet Kofi-Tsekpo

I am particularly interested in the impacts of language and ideology, their political and emotional fallout, and interdependence. For me, the personal and the political are always present in poetry, whether or not these elements are always apparent.

I've tried to use different voices in my work, for example using quotes or dramatic monologue. *Sentences or* 'The House at Eldridge Street' begins with a line borrowed from Ciaran Carson's 'Calvin Klein's Obsession', the poet himself quoting from 'Old Man' by Edward Thomas. In each case, scent and memory elope within an historical setting. The line, 'They *bleached* Turkey' later on in the sequence was picked up from someone shouting on the 36 bus several years ago. In the poem echoing the title of a Lowell poem borrowed from Chaucer, 'To Speak of the Woe that is in Marriage', I sought to refract the colonialist project through the family dynamic.

In 'The Stump', originally written as a sestina, there is a tension between free and formal verse. I'm exploring that tension both formally and politically; the interplay of freedom and resistance through lyric and narrative.

from Sentences or 'the House at Eldridge Street'

1 *The Borrowed Line*

I am trying to think what it is I am remembering *about you*
    after all these years, aside from the smell of sweat and leather from
                                the jacket
you lent me on our way back to my house, which I wore happily
    that night striding down Holland Park Avenue, picking up a grape
outside a greengrocer, striding carefree after our first kiss
    over which you'd fumbled while delivering the line
borrowed from your friend's parents – who hailed from the Sixties
    and believed in infidelity and free love,
the laws of which, in keeping with our age, we faithfully obeyed –
    that as soon as we begin, we begin to die.

2 *Iceland*

The mother lives at the top of the house in her tiny kitchen,
    ornaments peeping out of the steam above the old cooker,
the father in the basement under a deep pile of antiques and pieces
                             of machinery.
    Your bedroom is on the first floor where they occasionally meet outside
to argue, in English for my benefit. 'You murderer!'
    While you were out, I found the Japanese porn your mother picked up
during one of her cleaning jobs, which reads back-to-front, beginning
                         with the slim,
    breastless native bodies and culminating with a buxom Scandinavian,
legs splayed as if the quest for fire had finally been satisfied and she'd
                            fallen back
    with laughter, her silvery-blue eyes like small fish under water.

3 *His Father's Complaint*

It's a habit I can't break. Thirty years in one house
    and I'm dreaming of the Peloponnese,
but I won't go. I'm too faithful to this damp cellar,
    and would never leave my children,
not that there haven't been any offers. Ladies of stature,
    elegance and decency, widows with several properties,
even young girls locking for a father have held my hand
    for too long. Tell me I'm not a gentleman,
but to watch her makes my heart crumble. I refuse to finish the place –
    got rid of her surveyors. Now you hear her moaning upstairs.

4 *A Mother's Antidote*

Listen to the old man sitting on his pile of junk,
    telling our whole business to the neighbours.
You see what I put up with? And now I hear
    the voice of that young girl in my son's room, panting
and gurgling away in the early hours, bloody heathen.
    This morning I heard them shouting and the door go *bam* –
like us in the early days – and her crying, pathetic.
    Before you know it, my husband's up there with the coffee,
smelling like a poison. So I bring her some tea –
    sweet and milky, just as my boy would have it.

5 *Eldridge Street*

The neighbour is outside wearing a mossy négligée,
    her face as broad as a boab, saliva glistening
in the moonlight. They *bleached* Turkey, she mutters, bleached it.
    We rush past the rubble, chrysanthemums on the windowsill,
up the battered wooden staircase into the master bedroom.
    The four-poster bed is empty and sullen, sagging with mixed fortune,
the father's escape from civil war, the mother working as a seamstress,
    he pulling her towards him, a hot convenience. Nothing's moved.
Embroidered sheets wear a layer of dust grey as the night waves.
    It won't happen now, I say, the moment has passed.

Noli me Tangere

In his pink-yellow *salmah* he sees her,
screaming out. I see you, she says,
walking here alone. Just like that worm
split by the gardener's hoe,

spread across the grass,
struggling to be whole
there in the earth's damp spot.
Don't touch me, he says.

Her hands are golden fires;
they lick His feet.

To Speak of It

Something is freed under the unnatural light.
All tolerance gone, love's on a loose hinge.
He wants to crush those soft colonial cheeks,
their bare betrayal, her eyes grey with fright.

She'll return to suburbia, tugged back
like a lace curtain, sniffed at, her baby
reddening beneath the window frames,
gulping at the tut-tutting birds at twilight.

And something is swaddled forever here
in this tight room, within its walls of skin;
inside, a soft violence embedded,
like a bone invisibly misshapen.

Doctor Davis

He holds her up like glistening lichen;
examines the tiny earlobes, brown snails,

the toes, small grubs, the navel
shrinking back, a mussel

reflecting coloured surfaces of skin.
Here and there, bones protrude.

Something is tearing through the body's
soft channels. It will gnaw the air

like a grey beast and nothing
that moves or speaks will soothe it.

Beuckelaer reports from the biblical scene

after four paintings by Joachim Beuckelaer at the National Gallery

1 *Water*

A thousand fish found stranded in the middle
of a market town have had better days.

Hooked and gutted and sliding over
each other in barrels, they have the eyes

of humans who secretly worship nothing.
Some get a fair bit of attention

as they shimmy along the cobbled stones,
their mouths agape. Traders throw up their hands.

A man with long hair holds up two fingers,
says he knows nothing about it.

2 *Air*

Singing sea shanties to the empty waters,
half the sailors are longing for their wives;

courtyard women who wring the necks of birds.
They lost their flight some time ago. Talons

are removed from the foot of a falcon
that like a slovenly girl lies featherless

amongst the ordinary poultry, partridges
and guinea-fowl, and other wild game.

3 *Fire*

What we create are pale imitations;
this meat on the hob, these bodies hanging
over a flame. The fire gently nibbles

the trees of the forest. She lays down
her blanket like a vixen covering
her young. A volcano is just

an adolescent nosebleed, an eruption
that might disturb her parents; make them
wake up and feel the heat of their own making.

4 *Earth*

As if it had been lifted into the air
and dropped again, the earth
belches something sweet,

shedding and renewing
by mere circumstance
the rotten and the riches,

as we scoop vegetables in their packs
and ignore the cauliflowers, smiling
superfluously like maiden aunts.

Dead Wasp at the Side of the Pool

You with the terrible reputation,
how beautiful you were, your belly black and shining,
legs like honeysuckle tongues,

your tail full and flaccid. An hour ago
I watched you drown, man without parachute,
wings beaten under an *August* sun.

The Stump

We have turned a corner, heading out
          on the road, and discover the gulls
have taken it over. The little island
          that was once a wood is now just a tuft

of hair, with no walls of stone to protect it,
          and no face to give it character. The river

is a willowy giant on the river's
          pathway. Somehow we all have to pass here.
If we turned away now, we would have to
          reconsider everything and head back

to where we started, migrating birds
          without instinct. So we sit on a wall

waiting for the tide to go out. The walls
          are mossy and covered with river
debris. And then, like a tropical bird,
          the stump of a rainbow appears; right there,

on a crock of grass. Each time I turn
          my head to look, the stump gets brighter.

Katharine Kilalea

'The Boy with a Fire in his Boot' and 'The Conductor and the World in the Wallpaper' are part of a series of poems in which I was exploring the ideas of fairy tales – the peculiar mix of the frightening and the benign, the sense of estrangement, things not having the right proportion. When I first read 'The Conductor and the World in the Wallpaper' to a group of poets in a workshop, they found it comic, which was not at all my intention. The lines 'The Violins! The Violins!', felt a musical equivalent (for the conductor) of Kurtz's 'The Horror! The Horror!'

'Kolya's Nails' has to do with the feeling that other people can see things about you which are invisible to yourself. This is what the cows provide – an odd and penetrating way of seeing the self, as thought from the outside.

'Hennecker's Ditch' is best listened to with a kind of floating ear, not trying too hard to piece things together. There's no narrative, but I think that, in some ways, it may describe a kind of journey. I think it has something in common with the feeling of dread that 'something's going to happen but you don't know what it is'. In the same way, it's like a journey towards something which feels meaningful but ultimately unknowable.

The Boy with a Fire in his Boot

I

Once, there was a boy who burnt his foot.
The story began in the Tsitsikamma
on a farm in a forest where everything was asleep.

The bed heard first and the covers parted,
the curtains blinked (too old for all this rushing around),
and the farmers looked out

to see flames waving from the valley below
where, in the light of night,
trees swayed, arms akimbo,

like in some fiery disco.
A network of paths, torch-lit, came alive
as the nearby farmers arrived

armed with slopping buckets.
Vines snapped, bark peeled,
the smell of cedar was strong

and smoke ran from the trees
like a frightened dog.
The night let out a gruff and smoky cough.

Then the farmers wrung dry their hands.
They damped their rags and broomsticks
and began to beat it.

II

This is the crippled forest
But a fire will feed on anything.
It licked out, singeing twigs and birds

which stirred too late. The boy stood up.
He put on his gumboots. He put on his dressing gown.
Dark grasses tracked him –

their footprints led from the edge of the house
to the edge of the wood,
which was another place,

without men or mothers,
and the crispy trees were a warning
he didn't understand.

The boy looked at the fire.
It was bigger than him
and he didn't know it yet,

but it was so frightening
that he grew older just from looking at it.
And the fire, equally inquisitive,

lifted its own lantern
exposing the days and years ahead,
folded neatly beneath his skin.

Moths spat and crackled.
And then the boy's flat-cap lifted.
It was all that held him together,

and now it blew quickly away,
like matchsticks lit.
He was just a boy, running.

One eye melted.
One eye dripped
in the wind.

His spirit welled from the trees
in a clear, clean sap
which ran to dark stains on the soil.

He was just a boy, running
with a fire in his boot,
and he was lifting his legs like a deer.

III

Two fires, running
neither pursuing, neither pursued,
they passed through the grasses,

the leaf litter and queued-up trees
as the moon passed through
the smoky-clouds overhead

like love, which moves on,
as a finger passes through a candle,
unscathed.

A path cleared before him:
trees falling, branches surrendering
with cracks and peeps and pops.

He was burning
but he did not grow smaller like
a cigarette.

He was breathing,
but it hurt to breathe,
but he was made to breathe –

He was like the fire in that way,
the desire to throw open his mouth
and gulp back the sky,

the way birds float,
when they fly.
Fire plus fire.

This is how a fire is fought:
a damp finger circling a wine glass
to make it sing.

IV

The forest shattered.

What a glorious explosion.
Grey plumes fluttered up.
Birds and embers twinkling

in the sky! Air was all around.
The night was cheap and ashen.
And as the farmers began to leave,

the thin-necked trees rose,
open-mouthed to a dry, grey rain
that would fall for days.

Spiders sang like gondolas
through the blackened channel of trees
and something green,

something you couldn't really see
through the rheumy residue of smoke,
lifted itself, gingerly, and left.

Nothing sinister, I suspect.
Just a sunrise which arrived,
and in a passing gesture of kindness

tossed its spare change
– crisp, cold coppers, golds, oranges, reds –
into the black and barren clearing.

The Conductor and the World in the Wallpaper

The conductor waves his baton,
his tuxedo splits behind him.
One and two and three and four and...

the brass bangs, the woodwind whines,
the strings vie for the delicate sounds
he hears in his mind. *Pianissimo*, he pleads,

but the French Horn is grumbling
like a shiny digestive system.
And one and two and three and four...

The conductor turns from the rostrum.
From the auditorium, the chairs watch him.
For a moment, the world stops coughing
                          and shuffling around.

His breath is the hiss of a puncture.
His peeling leather case is packed, latched,
carted out to a winter night

waiting to escort him –
an old man wrapped in the wind,
an old man, scattering pigeons with his stick,

passing through the night
where trains pass methodically
beneath lanes hunched thick with leaves.

Then comes the click of the front door.
And we hear his heart taking off its coat.
His footsteps tread the carpeted stairs

The violins! The violins!
They had hinted at things to come
but the patterns on the wallpaper meant nothing
                          to him.

The ringing telephone,
the dripping tap, the crickets…
And when the curtains closed with a clash

it was a deafening, dull and defeated sound
which could not be drowned
when held against his body.

Kolya's Nails

All night, the quiet countryside was ruined by the sound
                              of Kolya's nails
to-ing and fro-ing from her water bowl on the melamine floor.

You're much too sensitive, said Jo, I slept like a log.
And so what? There's more comfort in a dog than sleep.

Early the next morning we went walking, just Kolya and I.
I walked slowly as though the air was thick.

I opened a stile at the fence and Kolya wriggled through
and ran ahead, scattering cows, gobbled up

almost immediately by the long, dewy grass, the mist.
If there was a short cut, it was not the route she discovered

but what came over me in her absence. I saw it in the cows,
how they came down to the fence where I was standing

– confused and crying for her in the howling way
we call to dogs – and stared. They looked at me

with their caviar eyes and chewed sideways,
as though I were something spectacular,

or something that didn't add up. She would come back,
the fool, she always did, like a springy branch.

Hennecker's Ditch

              I stood at the station
like the pages of a book
whose words suddenly start to swim.

Wow. The rain. Rose beetles.

Formal lines of broad-leaved
deciduous trees
ran the length of the platform.

Ickira trecketre stedenthal, said the train.
Slow down please, said the road.
Sometimes you get lucky, said the estate agent
        onto his mobile phone,
it all depends on the seller.

Dear Circus,
Past the thicket, through the window,
the painéd months are coming for us —

See the bluff, the headland, announcing
the presence of water.
See the moths...

The trees walk backwards into the dark.

★ ★ ★

Hello? Hello? The snow
comes in sobs.
Dogs sob.
Cars sob across town.

Dear Circus,
When you found me
I was a rickety house.

There was a yellow light and a blanket
    folded up on the stoep
and the yellow light – *Dear Circus* –
was a night-blooming flower.

We pushed a chest of drawers against the door.
It's nice now that the corridor's empty.
A necklace. Vacant. Light wrecked the road.

Dear Circus,
We took off our clothes
and did cocaine for three weeks.

The washing machine shook so badly
that a man asleep four floors down reached out
    to hold it:
Shut that dirty little mouth of yours…

                ★ ★ ★

Hennecker's Ditch.

You'll never find it, he said over dinner,
a black lobster and bottle of vinegar,
unless, unless…

Blackened,
the dog tilts his head from beneath
    the canopy of the Karoo tree.
Look at my face, he said. Can you see what
    I'm thinking?

A red jersey. Bot bot bot.
Several breezes.
Boats on the water were moving at different speeds.
The baker took a portable radio
    into the garden
to listen to the cricket
in the shade of the bougainvillea.
Tick-a-tick-ooh, tick-a-tick-ah.

It was cloudy but hot. We were moving
        as shadows.

Three times he came upstairs and made love to her
then went back down and read his book.
The air was blood temperature
        and the consistency of blood.

Look at my face, he said.
I see you. I see you. I see you
        in our murky bath
I see you in our black and white bath like a cat.

                        ★ ★ ★

Barbed wire around the fisheries.
A letter from the municipality
Come closer, sir. Step into my office.

Above the harbour, tin roofs and cranes.

Henry? he said.
Hello? Henry? he said.
What's been happening in Dog Town these days?
The Audi keys lay heavy on the table.
Aaaaah Henry, he said. How wonderful it is
        to see you.
The mists came down.
The moon was bright.
Collectors searched the night market
        with flashlights, and the wind outside,
with its slight chill, howled.
Henry, the breezes – they bolt across the open market
like meatballs, Henry,
like windmills, Henry,
like policemen, Henry, apprehending criminals...

A man in a collared shirt put a cigarette
        to his mouth
and looked at his watch.
And what happened then?

He wore a street hat. He wore a street hat and
    carried a belt over one arm.
And what happened afterwards?

Tell her… I think he has given up.
Tell her… I know now, this is what I've been afraid of
    all my life.

He closed the door and came in.
He closed the door and the sound of the bathwater dimmed.

★ ★ ★

Thirty-one back gardens.
Thirty-one back gardens overlooking
    the backs
of thirty-one houses.
Thirty-one houses looking out over the sea.
And the sea – *of course it was* – was marbled
    and contorting.

Are you sleeping? – Yes.
Figures in yellow mackintoshes make their way
    along the coastal path.
And then, what then if I were to ask,
How much longer?
If I were to say, How much further?
It's just
I have used up all my reserves.

There was a yellow light
and a blanket folded up on the stoep.
The light was burning dimly now.
By that time,
the light had begun to flicker.

He opened the door and fastened
    his lonely shadow,
and she fastened hers
and sat on the chair.

I think we are in the middle, aren't we.
He said, I think we may be.
We're certainly not at the beginning anymore.

★   ★   ★

The moon was acting strangely.
The moon was moving fast.
It was cloudy but hot.
Electricity cables gathered round a pole
like the roof of a marquee.

He wore a gold vagina on his chest.
He had gold lining on the flaps of his jacket.
She lay her head against the window and sang a song
    by Silvio Rodriguéz
wearing ten gold balls on a chain around her neck.
Dear Circus,
Sometimes we are just so full of emotion.

And what happened then?
And what happened afterwards?
Chicken bones and Pick 'n Pay receipts.
We were moving as shadows.
And the only light
    was the light from the bakery.

A lampshade swings above the window.
Tick-a-tick-ooh, tick-a-tick-ah
We have no history.
Nothing has passed between us.
A hundred years pass like this.

Dear Circus,
I need to see more glass!
I need to see more glass!
This has to be more gentle.

Jee Leong Koh

Where did these poems begin? They began on a horrible afternoon when my tutor in his room at Wadham College read aloud the sentences I plagiarised from some book on Ben Jonson. They began in the backroom of a bar. They began with quotations – word, form or spirit – of Eavan Boland, Pablo Neruda, Octavio Paz and Roland Barthes. They began before my wretched grandfather died and after I stopped believing in God. They began at a Frida Kahlo show, studied with half-averted gaze. They began as I walked away from a long-anticipated break-up, two shopping bags stuffed with clothes in each hand, tears watering both cheeks, a cliché on Broadway on a Sunday. So many beginnings. But I think these poems really began when I moved from Singapore to New York and came out, so to speak, as gay. Which is to say that these poems began from humiliation and went on their way.

Attribution

I speak with the forked tongue of colony.
Eavan Boland, 'The Mother Tongue'

My grandfather said life was better under the British.
He was a man who begrudged his words but he did say this.

I was born after the British left
an alphabet in my house, the same book they left in school.

I was good in English.
I was the only one in class who knew 'bedridden' does not mean lazy.

I was so good in English they sent me to England
where I proved my grandfather right

until I was almost sent down for plagiarism I knew was wrong
and did not know was wrong, because where I came from everyone
plagiarised.

I learned to attribute everything I wrote.
It is not easy.

Sometimes I cannot find out who first wrote the words I wrote.
Sometimes I think I wrote the words I wrote with such delight.

Often the words I write have confusing beginnings
and none can tell what belongs to the British, my grandfather or me.

A Whole History

In the morning they were both found dead.
Of cold. Of hunger. Of the toxins of a whole history.
Eavan Boland, 'Quarantine', Section IV of 'Marriage'

The floor is cold with the coming winter.
   I pull on white socks
and sit down before the blackout window
to think about our separation closing in.

We have a history longer than the two years
   that fitted like a shirt.
You learned a long time ago to enjoy ironing.
I always had someone ironing shirts for me.

But we go further back than birth, to furtive
   park encounters,
coded glances, tapping on bathroom walls,
ways of staying warm and white in winter.

Yesterday a young friend said it's wrong
   to expose children
to a gay wedding. The chill hit me again.
Rage spread like blood over my clean shirt.

I cannot wash it off. You are no longer willing.
   In the closet the shirt,
part reminder of love, part reminder of rage,
is held up by its shoulders on thin twisted wire.

The Rooms I Move In

the bay windbreak, the laburnum hang fire, feel
the ache of things ending in the jasmine darkening early
Eavan Boland, 'The Rooms of Other Women Poets'

I have moved in the rooms of other women poets
and, seeing African violets, checked if they needed water,

careful not to disturb the stolen time in the chairs,
the swivel leather seat, the one with a high cane back.

The desks, if there was one, were bright with circumstance
cast by an Anglepoise lamp, crooked, articulate.

The window might look out on an old monastery
but the door kept its ear open to a cry or a creak.

Such rooms I moved in when I move between the men
crowded with desire they disperse in a stranger's hand.

Before their face I offer the flower of my mouth,
red in the red light but also out of the red light,

a wild hibiscus impossible to label chaste
if my red mouth is not so chastened by my need.

from 'Seven Studies for a Self Portrait'

Study #5: After Frida Kahlo

I dream I am a wreck of a woman.

I am not grand like ruins, I am not a broken column.

I am the traffic accident on morning radio.

A bus handrail is sticking in my uterus like a huge thumbtack.

My collarbone hangs from my throat like a necklace.

I dream a monkey is picking up bits of my spine with his pale hands.

The monkey is carefully arranging me back together.

I hear the Professor say the monkey is the traditional symbol for lust.

My monkey is very gentle.

When he is finished, I will take him to my breast, and offer him my nipple.

Translations Of An Unknown Mexican Poet

Unless
I'm going to kill myself unless the day lets me in.
Every face is a closed door. Every tree is a curtain.
The smallheaded pigeon brings no message for me.
The bright air gives way but doesn't give entrance.

I think I have been walking for a very long while,
past tall chain fences, down smoked church aisles,
round and round the shrinking circle of a clock,
away from the turn of cliffs that I walk towards.

I'm going to the Brooklyn Bridge, to stop thinking
about fences and churches and clocks. I'm going
to the middle of the Bridge to throw myself over it
to find another door since the day won't let me in,

unless some tree decides to raise its blind an inch,
unless some bird, perhaps a gull, begins to sing.

Marriage

I'm married to the Mother of unbecoming sorrows.
I approach her like one would approach a shrine
smashed by boys throwing stones for ball practice.
What has a husband to do with sacred fragments?

I'm married to the Mother of unbecoming sorrows.
The children eat from bottles while the bone china
rattles from the cool dark of the heirloom dresser.
Tomorrow, yes, tomorrow, I will trash the plates.

She was a girl, once, green as a stalk of grass
I held between my teeth. She was the dew, once,
translucent sun on the tip of the stalk of grass
I bit into. She was the sweet, once, in the grass,

now she's the Mother of unbecoming sorrows
I'm married to, I'm married to, I'm married to.

The Corner

After the dark has leaned in the corner for hours,
the corner of the kitchen where I sat to write,
the notebook opened like a souvenir matchbook
down to its last match, the ashtray on my right;

after the dark has looked for hours from the corner
of her eye, has looked pale, lovely, almost white
under her translucent sheath, her mouth a startling
ruby, her ring catching the history of moonlight;

after the dark has listened for corners in the hours,
has listened for the figure in the formless night,
the *ranchera* in the blood repeating its black plea
for an inhabitable country out of human sight;

I strike my last match and the dark comes to me.
The flame looks and looks, and then it fails to see.

No One

No one is reporting the mysterious package
left in the middle of the packed train platform
but everyone round the package must have seen
the red gift paper tied up with a thread of string.

No one must get hurt, least of all my Rocio,
breathing like a newborn in her big new bed,
white breast unbuttoned by her pink pajamas
and cupped by the night air's big warm hands.

No one hears the rattle, the metal rush, the brake
that powers the engines of my head, the crowd
driving from every direction towards the door –
body stiffened to a point – before pushing off.

Someone has to see the mysterious package.
Someone has to say something to the cops.

The Pocket

This house has not grown too tight for Juan yet
nor too last season for a new sense of the world,
but the discontented walls provide no pockets
for halfchewed gum, a shiny quarter, hands.

And the boy is searching for pockets everywhere.
Not the room shared with his sister, not the bed
which sheds its blue cotton skin without warning,
not even the body turning out its impulsive pouch.

Soon he will find the silver lining in the mind,
a seam we follow like a suture, then a scar,
and then an igneous ridge on which genius runs,
scrambling and scraping some, to the very head

and see the chewedup jungle and the shiny cities
kept safe and secret in the pocket of the palm.

The Pigeon

Even the light crumples in this city, let alone
the takeout menus thrust from street corners,
the flowers bandaged in cellophane, the fire
escapes, the fatlidded women on the train.

In some back kitchen the men are crumbling
a bag of peas into the soup. In some back alley
the washing machines are muttering distractedly.
The light is still trying to straighten its wrinkles.

This is not a rat ironed flat on the road. This is
a pigeon. See the wings flattened out to feather.
See the white fluff still not completely blackened.
Affixed to the ground, the animal ruffles the light.

Hard to tell the difference but it is a pigeon.
Hard to tell the difference but it is still bright.

The Night

The storm blew out the trees, and night became the night
all of the dark crossed the dark. The mountain heaved
to stony feet and climbed the straining rope of a track,
hand over hand over hand over hand over hand over hand.

The ground the mind rests on and dreams of thinking,
the water the river feeds to generous and gated pipes,
the fire the house subdues from lightning and burns,
the air the body breathes without breathing: all gone.

The mountain clambered
                    and we hung off its back,
a rope curling from waist to waist to waist to waist
to an empty noose that hanged straight by its weight.

The storm blew out the trees, and night became the night
all of the dark crossed the dark, on Christmas night.

from 'A Lover's Recourse'

You look into a stone and see its early fire.
You look into a fire and all you see is fire.

The reason that we saw each other only twice
is that I have no hands to thrust into the fire.

Time is a river. That is if you are a fish.
If you are a sunflower, time is a fire.

We do not ever know what the gods want of us.
Perhaps that is why we compare them to fire.

A charred library is sadder than a pile of ash.
A body catches but it does not cage a fire.

Saying it makes no difference to the universe
but when did saying anything put out a fire?

Sick of analogies, Jee wants the thing itself.
What are you, Love, when you are not a fire?

★

Among the ways to take a good look at a tree,
the best is to lie down and look up at a tree.

I can no more hold you by naming qualities
than sacred names etched in the bark possess the tree.

All that I touch of you are touches and not you.
A torn branch does not make the tree less of a tree.

Your life – your speed – moves independently of mine.
Looking elsewhere does not hasten or slow the tree.

Being is your glory, which no one can take from you,
unless they take you down, for burial, from the tree.

The angel of despair, the demon of desire,
the many leaves that flutter on a lonely tree.

Jee, lay your anguish on the ground and look up.
The tree. The sky. The tree. The sky held by the tree.

★

I close the door but the day climbs in through a window.
Other days long thought dead follow it through the window.

Mad with us – or with dad – you turned us out. We walked
and turned but could not see your face at the small window.

You wheeled your bike past the window, and Dad was home.
I circled, with metallic clicks, the five o'clock window.

The windows, grilled to baffle body, locked us out,
but a wire finger opened the door through a window.

To cut my losses I chalk round me an endless circle.
To stop the train from crashing in I close the window.

Inside the restaurant, I watched you hurry in,
watched you, first, through the window, then, without the window.

Jee gives his dad the name of love, his mum, of loss.
She closed the door on us but, Love, he cleaned the windows.

★

You smell your fault as readily as you hear a bell.
Ignorance rings a school bell, ego a church bell.

The loop of wire moves along the twist of wire.
Steady your hand or desire will sound the bell.

I ache for the beautiful young men I pass on streets.
They do not know they are beautiful bronze bells.

Out of the party chatter rises a cathedral.
My tongue keeps ringing my head that is the bell.

He has heard of, but has not heard, the onehand clap.
He has tapped many bodies but has not heard the bell.

I hope perfection does not lie in quietness.
A poet builds his house in the fading of a bell.

The fading is a fault but silence is an itch.
Most unendurable, Jee, is the unrelenting bell.

Julith Jedamus

When I saw Drenthe, in deep February snow, I knew I had to write about it. The thatched farmhouses, the brick roads lined with leafless poplars, the linseed mill, the frozen canals: all made a deep impression. For days after I returned I tried to find the right form. I wanted something quiet and plain – something that suited the horizontal landscape, and the land that seemed so perdurable yet was so clearly under threat. I thought I'd try a syllabic, for the discipline of it. But it was only when I came upon the hook-and-eye slant-rhymes that I knew I had a poem.

Form need not be a constraint. It is a partner to spar with. Rules can be broken or bent. Patterns can be distorted, perverted, transformed. But the form must fit the thought. Even in free verse this is true. Closed forms simply require more manoeuvres. There is more to take on, or to fight against.

I wrote 'Fixed Form' (which is partly about the Snow Queen, and partly about Hans Christian Andersen, that cold-eyed master of psychological cruelty) in answer to those who accuse the 'new formalists' of living in a prison of their own making. Do they want to escape? Should they? Who can say?

In Memory of the Photographer Wilson 'Snowflake' Bentley, Who Died of Pneumonia after Walking through a Blizzard Near Jericho, Vermont, December 23, 1931

Beauty was, for him, cold,
hexagonal, perfect
in all its parts, beheld

once and once only. Locked
beneath his lens, light-spun
and light-refracting, flecked

with coal dust and pollen,
his flakes shone with lunar
loveliness... And we can

see, in these hundred-year-
old prints, plain evidence
of his attention, care,

and chilling confidence:
in the manifold world,
its willed evanescence,

its subtle signs and wild
and blinding storms. Did it
surprise him, to be killed

by a surfeit of white –
a blazing increment
of stars, ferns, wands and bright

escutcheons, an argent
army of perfectness?
Look, and see his wind-bent

back, his boots caked with ice,
his glazed eyes... Did he have,
in his last seditious

delirium, one brave
black thought: did God murder
us all with too much love?

Van Gogh in Drenthe

He walks the cinder path, head crooked, oil-coat flapping,
boots soaked from yesterday's storm, canvas and campstool
under one arm. Pockets stuffed with tobacco and chalk, paint tubes
rattling in a rain-streaked box. He stops, scents colour as a hound
scents fox. Draws a grid, stabs at his palette, scolds staring
turf-cutters. Works for hours. Forgets to eat. Breathes the immense
autumn twilight, its seriousness. He's one of the watchers. He sees:

Rood: Brick ovens in russet orchards. Glow of peat, smear
of sunrise. A girl's shawl. His bloodshot eyes (he bathes them in tea).

Groen: Drenched grass. Sod cottages roofed with moss. Near Zweeloo,
seas of winter wheat. He feels himself take root in sooty soil:

Zwart of earth, of wet bark, of a crêpe-wrapped headdress worn
by a Frisian widow, of locks and wharves, and peat-barges drawn

by white horses. *Bleek* canals and fields of hail, pallid faces
of weed-burners and potato-diggers, hands knotting bleached laces.

Grijs: Skies of slate and palest lilac, their iridescence
unsurpassed by oil; light unrenderable, its deliquescence

visible and invisible, merging with mist and rain. High clouds
shifting and ravelling between azure gleams: *Hemelsblau*.

Geel of candles indoors and lanterns without, of comforts shunned, gold
flowers not yet seen, letters not yet written – the last blood-soiled.

The Cull

Last night I heard gunshots in Richmond Park,
but my November mind, thick with smoke
    and fear of wars
and phantom men, mistook the reason:
the cull of bucks and stags after the rutting season,
    when mast is scarce.

At dawn I walked through Bog Gate, and found
nothing: no drag mark, no blood on the ground,
    no trace of violence.
Mist threaded red bracken, and the broken ridge
of pollard oaks that march towards Holly Lodge
    and its sharp defence.

By the track they call Deane's Lane I saw him:
a twelve-point stag, his scraped horns trimmed
    with moss and bracken,
his hindquarters lean, one shin gored and clotted.
I watched him browse, and waited for a quickening, an unseen sign –
    his, the day's, mine.

Fixed Form

There's a sliver in my eye.
    My heart is cold.
Children cannot rescue me
    with tears that scald.

Blue auroras light the panes
    of my prison.
Driven crystals pierce my veins
    with precision.

Etched upon an icy lake

old patterns shine.
Love's reversals cannot make
their meanings mine.

What malice cramped my hand?
Who fixed my form?
I wish a lime-scented wind
would make me warm.

Admetus, Alcestis

after Herbert

He strokes her hair,
breathes her beauty,
carries her up the stair
to the bed where she wept for duty,
drops her shroud onto a chair.

What groves
of words, what incensed lines
save these lovers' loves?
What unveiled truth gains
from praise at two removes?

Stowing a Single in Furnivall Boathouse on the Chiswick Mall

In memory of A.J.H.

Andy, I still see
you hoisting the Swift
onto your shoulder,
balancing it up
the ramp, pausing at
the tide-boards, swinging
one long leg over,
then the other – your
Aigles streaked with mud,
your bare knees steady –
crossing the pavement,
nudging the bow-ball
through the bright green doors,
angling the single
up to the rack – breath
held as you eased its
rigger round – stowing
it safely, glancing
at me with your pale
startling eyes, never
mentioning my fears
or mistakes, simply
saying, in your off-
hand way, 'Cup of tea?
Put the kettle on,
and I'll grab our blades.'

Snow Is Not Celibate

Snow is not celibate.
Its errors, though immense,
are seldom permanent,
its indiscriminations
just. Efforts must
be made to understand
its point of view. Who
can fault its consummate
deceptions? White lies
are socially acceptable,
and as for the howlers –
snow was always prone
to exaggeration. Its talent
for melodrama was clear
from the start. As for that
domineering streak, no efforts,
chemical or otherwise,
could tame it. Who can change
a blizzard's nature? Better
to take snow as it is:
cold, manipulative, manic
at times, profoundly antisocial...
Yet beneath its crusty
exterior abides a pure
and succouring soul – a soul
to melt the hardest heart,
stanch the deepest doubt.

The White Cliff

This is the face of England, sheer and plain,
the book read backwards, the sugar-loaf,
the main, the high plucked forehead of a queen,
the cracked wall of a citadel. Half
of me believed this, and half did not,
as I walked its furzy crown one night
in June, the metaphoric rock beneath my feet
felt, not seen, and cliffs to the west bright
as lace, festooned with fissures and gaudy
similes. At sunrise, a gull rose above the face,
and I wished for its literal eyes... And I thought of
my rebellious ancestors, who left this place
for a more austere one. After they had gone,
the cliffs, unconscious, shone and shone...

Belle Tout

Beautiful, futile: a flash, then darkness. Cliff-
bound, cliff-threatened, your housed light
drenched in cloud, your minatory face half-
seen, half-guessed: what's this, that
led men not to safety but their graves?
Silent siren, beacon to the dreaming drowned,
who could have guessed your motive? Lives
were your trophy. Below, waves wound
themselves on the shingle, and white cliffs rise,
cancelling your beauty. How fortunate when,
a century past your founding, you were prised
from the cliff-edge and moved inland, drawn
on oiled rails. Now, blind and disarmed,
you guard the green endangered downs.

The Drowning of Drenthe

I travelled to a level land
Past sleeping towns with names of sand:
    Now they are gone.

The polders from the marshes won,
The houses made of brick not stone:
    Raise no alarm.

The linseed mill with icy arms,
The whitewashed churches purged of charms
    Evade our look.

The beeches smooth as vellum books,
The storks and blackbirds, doves and rooks
    Are rare as rare.

The coffee urns, the *huis-vrouw* cheer,
The biscuits furled like the New Year:
    The guests are late.

Bronze dagger, pin and carcanet,
Twice-strangled girl rescued from peat
    Bright waves obscure.

The tower wet with widows' tears,
The lion weltered in cold lairs
    Cannot be traced.

I hear the cries from each high place
As it rose up, victorious:
    The rampant sea.

The past is new, the future old;
Who can say now what rhymes are told
    In this drowned world?

John Dennison

Many of these poems have their origins in some experience of being transported, literally: family members' travels through South-East Asia and Europe by train, plane and bicycle; a car ride through the Otago night across the Taieri plain towards Dunedin; an early morning train from Leuchars across the Firth of Forth to Edinburgh. Something of the strangeness of being transported, particularly by train, found its way into the emotional shape of these poems too – that odd combination of suspense, of a holding, with fluid, inexorable motion. And being transported, and the poem's simultaneous suspension and movement, frequently finds me returning to certain coordinates: to place, to the importance of particularity, and to the question of relief, of our turning, of Grace and our refusals. These are some of those things which, as the wedding pantoum 'The Garden' puts it, bear repeating.

Northwards

In the way I stall
under the oncoming headlight
of each ancient train,

this acupuncture of light,
the weightless years that advance,
recede, the dot-to-dot surveillance

of our listless twitching, driving.
Off the surface of Waihola
they cover us.

There is relief only in waiting
for the rind to roll under us,
a brief valve in our atmospheres.

Who moves? Do we rear earthily
into the black Taieri hills, or does Orion,
his blue diamonds worn long over cool indigo,

slip into the wings?

To Keep Warm Inside

Under the bitter yoke
of these red untempered mornings,

steer the car like a life-raft
down Cumberland to this

crystal palace, this sometime church.
Tiles, and the wall of light

steaming across the variegated
blues of February.

The liquid aisles, lightly ushering,
rope the depth beneath,

declining order: fast,
medium, slow; aquajoggers

descend and return
shallow from deep. Receive

the goggled epiphany: limbs
flaying out the imagined ellipse, torsos

strapped just buoyant below the surface,
striving for peace or perfection,

in Dunedin – steamed open like a cockle
this morning in mid-July.

Nocturne

Drawn in the shallow breath of the night,
I wait for you to come back home,
willing the shadows to find your form;

but how can they carry your bright step,
the house of light that is your face?
My lighthouse, my love, the rocks are night all around.

Standing on the porch, I drive these backroads –
some hurt unwinding, some dry-mouthed valley,
and the sounds – drab, surd syllables:

the cough of a sheep;
the hills, their sodden bails as they slump;
small branches fret the roofing iron.

Turn heart, turn – go back home;
leave this road unwound.

Reed

Isa. 42:3

To turn here, rain brightening the trail
ahead, and stand, thoughts shaking and lame –
my doubtful fingers read the bole-cast braille
where some king of fools cut his name;
slow fire: see how the sap's running mirth
must stigmatise us – we bleed to grow.
Tall – a scaffold lifting from the earth,
sky-thrasher, a swelling of shadow –
now, torn, tongues let loose, the shattered crown
pours out its rushing supplication;
fleshy grasses, outstripping the ground,
run blindly from the flaming, from
the wind that scores its song in us and
this tree – *our Father!* – clapping its hands.

Source to Sea

for Rebekah and Mark

What is this turning mystery,
this juncture, this opening in the land?
Love traces the river from source to sea,
the distance covered in the joining of your hands.

This juncture, this opening in the land
a train draws itself through, inexorably,
the distance covered. In the joining of your hands
the track leaps ahead to fresh inland seas –

a train draws itself through. Inexorably,
the walled city reveals its gardens; now found,
the track leaps ahead to fresh inland seas,
lanes where coupling bicycles unwind.

The walled city reveals its gardens now. Found
wandering together, visiting love's untidy
lanes where coupling bicycles unwind,
you will camp in each other's mercy.

Wandering together, visiting love's untidy
red telephone boxes, you understand
you will camp in each other's mercy.
All this movement: lips meet; you find

red telephone boxes; you understand
love traces the river. From source to sea,
all this – movement – lips meet – you find
what is this turning mystery.

Watermarks

for Claire Beynon

Engines ahead of us and we're drawn,
another journey beginning in darkness;

we go through the cutting,
faces half-selving on the double glazing –

now fading into the slate dawn.
The train's refrain picks up –

particular, particular, particularly –
as everything waxes,

bruised light letting down
on wet hollows, fields harrowed, wheat on the turn.

Eyes follow the soft verge,
a certain line of questioning falling over

hedges, grounded rooks,
sheds, suggestions of thresholds;

and always engines ahead,
the thudding haul as we hug the embankment.

Black sycamores, and the pale green arrangements
of caravans give out,

the firth blurring into view –
a charcoal feathering of sight,

furthering over the immaculate surface:
all gradation, all meniscus,

fine grit and water,
sea holding weed holding stone holding

our brief gaze wavering along the lines,
and the morning lifts into the opaque horizon:

light's hesitations at the pointedness of everything.
People on the beach pause and stare again –

a train passing above water,
a fine hand drawn across paper,

sky heavy above with water,
and herring gulls cry in the wheels.

The Garden

for Paul and Maddie

You step from the house into the garden;
the light gathers in your wake
and lets loose, falling across the kitchen
threshold. In the summer dusk,

the light gathers in. You wake
as you home across London's
threshold in the summer dusk,
into the sanctuary, a promise held open

for you – home across London
to sit down at the table together. Now you walk
into the sanctuary: a promise held open,
the joining of hands – love speaks

and sits down at the table. Together now you walk
the walls of a small garden; nothing to darken
the joining of hands. Love speaks:
some things bear repeating, and those things lighten

the walls of a small garden, nothing to darken
you sitting to write, dream, seek
those things that bear repeating. And something lightens
as you gather folk and make them welcome – there is joy to mark

you setting dreams to rights. Seek,
and let loose. Calling across the kitchen
you gather folk and make welcome. Here, then, is joy to mark
you. Step from the house into the garden.

Author Biographies

SHERI BENNING grew up on a small farm in Saskatchewan, Canada. She has since travelled widely while attaining several academic degrees. She published two books of poetry in Canada, *Thin Moon Psalm* (Brick Books, 2007) and *Earth After Rain* (Thistledown Press, 2001). Her poetry, essays and fiction have also appeared in Canadian literary journals and anthologies. At work on new poems and a novel, Benning divides her time between Glasgow, Scotland, and a farm near Manitou Lake, Saskatchewan.

TARA BERGIN was born in Dublin in 1974. She is currently studying at Newcastle University for a PhD on Ted Hughes's translations of János Pilinszky. Her poems have appeared in *Poetry Review*. *Poetry London*, *Modern Poetry in Translation* and *PN Review*.

DAN BURT was born in South Philadelphia in 1942. He attended state schools and a local catholic college before reading English at Cambridge. He graduated from Yale Law School and practised law in the United States, United Kingdom and Saudi Arabia until moving to London in 1994 and becoming a British citizen. He is an honorary Fellow of St John's College Cambridge and lives and writes in London. His poetry publications include the Lintott pamphlets *Searched for Text* (2008) and *Certain Windows* (2011), and *Cold Eye*, a poetry and image collaboration with the artist Paul Hodgson (Marlborough, 2010).

JOHN DENNISON was born in Sydney in 1978. He grew up in Tawa, New Zealand, and studied English literature at Victoria University of Wellington and the University of Otago. He recently completed a PhD at the University of St Andrews on the prose poetics of Seamus Heaney and now lives with his family in Wellington.

WILL EAVES was born in Bath in 1967. He is the author of three novels, *The Oversight* (2001), *Nothing To Be Afraid Of* (2005) and *This Is Paradise* (2012, forthcoming), all published by Picador. His chapbook of poems, *Small Hours*, appeared in 2006. For many years he was the Arts Editor of the *Times Literary Supplement*. He now teaches in the Department of English at the University of Warwick. His first collection, *Sound Houses* (Carcanet), appeared in 2011.

MINA GORJI was born in Tehran and grew up in London. She is a lecturer in the English Faculty at Cambridge University and a fellow of Pembroke College. Her published work includes a study of John Clare and essays on awkwardness, mess, weeds and rudeness. Her poems have appeared, among other places, in *Magma*, *PN Review*, *The London Magazine* and *The International Literary Quarterly*.

OLI HAZZARD was born in Bristol in 1986. His poetry has appeared or is forthcoming in magazines and anthologies including *The Forward Book of Poetry 2010*, *The Best British Poetry 2011* and *The Salt Book of Younger Poets*. He studied English at University College London and is currently a graduate student at Bristol University.

JULITH JEDAMUS grew up in the mountains west of Boulder, Colorado. For the past sixteen years she has lived in London. She began writing novels, switched to short stories, and now writes verse. Her first collection, *The Cull*, will be published by Carcanet in 2012.

EVAN JONES was born in Toronto and now lives in Britain. He has a PhD in English and Creative Writing from the University of Manchester and has taught at York University in Toronto, and in Britain at the University of Bolton and Liverpool John Moores University. His first collection, *Nothing Fell Today But Rain* (Fitzhenry & Whiteside Ltd, 2003), was a finalist for the Governor General's Literary Award for Poetry. His second collection, *Paralogues*, is forthcoming with Carcanet.

Originally from South Africa, KATHARINE KILALEA moved to London in 2005 to study for an MA in Creative Writing at the University of East Anglia. Her first book, *One Eye'd Leigh* (Carcanet, 2009), was shortlisted for the Costa Poetry Award and longlisted for the Dylan Thomas Prize for writers under thirty. She works part-time as a publicist for an architecture practice in London.

HENRY KING was born in Bedford in 1987, and grew up in France and Surrey. He now lives in Glasgow, where he is studying for a PhD in English Literature at the University of Glasgow. In 2007, his family moved to Vancouver, which he occasionally visits.

JANET KOFI-TSEKPO's writing has appeared in anthologies and journals, including *Ten* (Bloodaxe, 2010), *Red* (Peepal Tree, 2010), *Bittersweet* (The Women's Press, 1998), *Wasafiri* and *Poetry Review*. She was one of the participants on The Complete Works programme run by Spread the Word, and lives in London.

JEE LEONG KOH is the author of three books of poems, including his most recent *Seven Studies for a Self Portrait*. Born and raised in Singapore, he read English at Oxford University, took his MFA in Creative Writing at Sarah Lawrence College, and now lives in New York City.

WILLIAM LETFORD lives in Stirling, Scotland, and works as a roofer. He has received a New Writer's Award from the Scottish Book Trust, was the recipient of an Edwin Morgan Travel Bursary from the Arts Trust of Scotland, and has an M.Litt. (Distinction) in Creative Writing from Glasgow University.

VINCENZ SERRANO is working on a PhD in Creative Writing and English and American Studies at the University of Manchester. Before this, he taught in Ateneo de Manila University, where he was coordinator for undergraduate studies in literature. His book, *The Collapse of What Separates Us*, was published by High Chair in 2010. It won first prize for poetry in the Carlos Palanca Memorial Awards for Literature (Philippines) in 2009.

HELEN TOOKEY was born near Leicester in 1969. She studied philosophy and literature at university and has worked in academic publishing, as a university teacher, and as a freelance editor. Her short collection *Telling the Fractures*, a collaboration with photographer Alan Ward, was published by Axis Projects in 2008.

LUCY TUNSTALL was born in London in 1969 and now lives in Bristol. She is a doctoral student at the University of Exeter working on the poetry of Dickinson, Moore, Bishop and Plath. Her poems have appeared in *PN Review*.

ARTO VAUN was born in Cambridge, Massachusetts and has attended Harvard University, Glasgow University, and the University of Massachusetts, Boston. He has contributed to *The Verb* (BBC 3), and is currently a contributing editor for *Glimpse Journal*. He has taught writing, literature and critical thinking. He is also a songwriter and musician, performing under the monikers Mishima USA and The Kent 100s. His first collection, *Capillarity*, was published by Carcanet in 2010; his next collection of poems is entitled *Isinglass*.

DAVID C. WARD is an historian at the National Portrait Gallery, Smithsonian Institution, where he has curated exhibitions on Walt Whitman and Abraham Lincoln, among others. With graduate degrees from Warwick and Yale Universities, he is the author of *Charles Willson Peale, Art and Selfhood in the Early Republic* (2004) and (with Jonathan D. Katz) *Hide/Seek: Difference and Desire in American Portraiture* (2010). He is currently working on an exhibition called *Poetic Likeness: Portraits of American Poets* that will open at the NPG in Autumn 2012. His pamphlet of poems *Internal Difference* was published by Lintott Press in 2011.

RORY WATERMAN was born in Belfast, grew up mostly in rural Lincolnshire, and currently lives in Bristol. His poems have appeared in *Stand*, *Agenda*, the *Times Literary Supplement*, *PN Review*, *The Bow-Wow Shop* and various other publications, and he co-edits *New Walk Magazine*.

JAMES WOMACK (Cambridge, 1979) studied Russian and English at university, and has lived in St Petersburg, Moscow and Conil de la Frontera. He currently lives in Madrid, where he teaches English Literature at the Universidad Complutense and with his wife runs Nevsky Prospects, a publishing house which produces Spanish translations of Russian literature. His first collection will be published by Carcanet in 2012.

ALEX WYLIE was born in Blackpool in 1980 and grew up on Lancashire's Fylde coast. In 2004 he moved to Belfast to undertake doctoral research at Queen's University, writing a thesis on T.S. Eliot and Geoffrey Hill. He currently teaches in the School of English at Queen's University Belfast and is co-editor of the online magazine *Poetry Proper*.

Acknowledgements

Sheri Benning
'Fidelity', 'That song that goes' and 'Listen' were published in Benning's collection *Thin Moon Psalm* (Toronto: Brick Books, 2007). 'Near the River', 'Plainsong', 'Dusk' and 'Vigil' previously appeared in *PN Review*.

Tara Bergin
'This is Yarrow' first appeared in *Poetry London* 56. 'Portrait of the Artist's Wife as a Younger Woman', 'Rapeseed', 'You Could Show a Horse', 'Questions', 'Military School', 'Red Flag', 'Swiss Station Room' and 'If Painting Isn't Over' were published in *PN Review*. 'Himalayan Balsam for a Soldier' appeared in *Modern Poetry in Translation* (3:6, 2006).

Dan Burt
'Who He Was' and 'Un Coup de Des' appeared in *PN Review* and in Burt's second chapbook, *Certain Windows* (Lintott Press, 2011); 'Trade' appeared in *Certain Windows*. 'Manque' was first published in *The Eagle*; 'Sie Kömmt' appeared in Burt's first chapbook, *Searched For Text* (Lintott Press, 2008), and in his collaborative book with the artist Paul Hodgson, *Cold Eye* (Marlborough Graphics/Lintott Press, 2010). 'Ishmael' was published in *Searched For Text*, *Cold Eye* and *Certain Windows*. 'Un Coup de Des', 'Manque', 'Sie Kömmt' and 'Ishmael' were all recorded for the Poetry Archive.

John Dennison
'Reed', 'Watermarks' and 'Source to Sea' were published in *PN Review*. An earlier version of 'Reed' was published in *Critic*. 'Source to Sea' was first published in *Deep South;* 'Watermarks' and 'To Keep Warm Inside' were first published in the *Otago Daily Times*.

Will Eaves
'From Weymouth' originally appeared in *The New Yorker*; 'Charity' in the *Times Literary Supplement*; 'Accommodation for Owls', 'Any Impediment', 'Three Flies' and 'Elegies Around Noon' were all published in *PN Review* and 'A Year Later' was broadcast on BBC Radio 3's *The Verb*. All of the poems appear in Eaves's first collection, *Sound Houses* (Carcanet, 2011).

Mina Gorji
'Empire of the Dandelion', 'Bittern', 'Be consoled' and 'Pitseolak' first appeared in *PN Review*. 'Kamasutra (the subsidiary arts)' was published in *Magma* and *The International Literary Quarterly*; 'Serenade' was published in *The International Literary Quarterly*. 'The art of escape' appeared in *The Delinquent*; 'Pearl Diver' appeared in *Oxford Magazine* and *The International Literary Quarterly*.

Oli Hazzard
'Moving In' previously appeared in *PN Review* and *The Forward Book of Poetry 2010*; 'Sonnet' appeared in *PN Review* and *Best British Poetry 2011*, and 'A Walking Bird' in *PN Review*. 'True Romance' and 'The Inability to Recall the Precise Word for Something' were published in *Poetry Salzburg Review*; 'Prelude to Growth' and 'Apologia' in *Clinic II*.

Julith Jedamus
'The Drowning of Drenthe' was published in *The New Yorker*. 'In Memory of the Photographer Wilson 'Snowflake' Bentley, Who Died of Pneumonia after Walking through a Blizzard Near Jericho, Vermont, December 23, 1931', 'The White Cliff' and 'Fixed Form' have appeared in *PN Review*.

Evan Jones
'Cavafy in Liverpool' and 'Bundesland Bavaria, Between Deffingen and Denzingen' appeared in *Agni*; 'Little Notes On Painting' appeared in *The SHOp*; 'Prayer to Saint Agatha' appeared in *PN Review*; 'God in Paris, 1945' appeared in *Malahat Review*; 'Actaeon' appeared in *New Quarterly*; 'Black Swallows from the Desert' appeared in *The Wolf*.

Katharine Kilalea
'The Boy with a Fire in his Boot' appeared in *PN Review* and subsequently in Kilalea's first collection of poems, *One Eye'd Leigh* (Carcanet, 2009). 'The Conductor and the World in the Wallpaper' and 'Kolya's Nails' appeared in *One Eye'd Leigh*. 'Hennecker's Ditch' was commissioned for broadcast on BBC Radio 3's *The Verb* and later published in *PN Review*.

Henry King
'Two Goodbyes' was first published in *TYPE Review* (Glasgow). 'Vancouver', 'Agnostic Epigrams' and 'A Windower' have appeared in *New Walk*.

Janet Kofi-Tsekpo
The poems included in *New Poetries V* have not previously been published.

Jee Leong Koh
'Attribution', 'A Whole History', 'The Rooms I Move In', 'Translations Of An Unknown Mexican Poet' and 'from *A Lover's Recourse*' were first published in *PN Review*. The extract from *Seven Studies for a Self Portrait* appeared in *Ganymede* (Issue Four, June 2009).

William Letford
'By the time we met' appeared in *Poetry Scotland*; 'It's aboot the labour' and 'Taking a headbutt', were first published by the Scottish Book Trust. The poet would like to thank the Linda Jackson Band for recording 'Sunday, with the television off', on their album, *Solitary Refinement*.

Vincenz Serrano
All of these poems appeared in Serrano's first collection, *The Collapse of What Separates Us*, published by High Chair (Quezon City, Philippines, 2010). Some of the poems have appeared or are forthcoming in the following publications: *High Chair* ('Static'), *Kritika Kultura* ('Short Walks') and *An Anthology of English Writing in Southeast Asia* ('Cornerhouse').

Helen Tookey
'Among Alphabets' was published in *PN Review* and then in *Telling the Fractures* (Axis Projects, 2008); 'At Burscough, Lancashire' was first published in *The Reader* and then in *Telling the Fractures*; 'Prints' and 'America' have appeared in *PN Review*; 'Start with this gesture' and 'Cockleshells' were published in *The Bow-Wow Shop* 6; 'With Joe on Silver Street' was published in *Poetry Wales* (46.1: summer 2010); 'Estuarine' and 'Climbing the Hill at Sunset' were first published in *Telling the Fractures*.

Lucy Tunstall
The poems which appear in *New Poetries V* have not been published previously.

Arto Vaun
'Father and Son in Orbit (July 1969)' appeared in *Matter 10*. 'Capillarity I', 'Capillarity XXVIII', 'Capillarity XLI' and 'Capillarity XLVII' were published in *PN Review* and subsequently in Arto Vaun's first collection, *Capillarity* (Carcanet, 2009). 'Capillarity XLVII' was also published in *The Forward Book of Poetry 2010*.

David C. Ward
'Def: Extreme Rendition', 'Colossus', 'The End of History', 'The River

Refuses its Name', 'Still we pretend at modesty', 'No Place', 'Surplus Value', 'Relict', 'Aces and Eights' and 'Two San Francisco Poets' were all published in *PN Review*. 'Clothes Make the Man' was published in *Poem* (Huntsville, Alabama); 'Teleology' was published in *Plainsongs* (Hastings College, Hastings, Nebraska).

Rory Waterman
'Family Business', 'Keepsakes' and '53.093336°N latitude / 0.253420°W longitude: 07/2010 capture: street view' first appeared in *The Bow-Wow Shop*. 'Nettles' first appeared in *Stand*. 'Out to the Fen', 'Distance', 'Ireland, 10', 'Driftwood', 'Winter Morning, Connecticut', 'A Suicide' and 'Back in the Village' first appeared in *PN Review*. 'The Lake' first appeared in *Orbis*. 'What Passing Bells' and 'For My Father' first appeared in *Able Muse*.

James Womack
'Complaint', 'The Dogs of a House in Mourning and the Naked Girl', 'Tourism', '"Don't Look Back, Lonesome Boy"', Experiment', 'Vomit' and 'La chute de la maison Usher' were all published in *PN Review*; 'Balance' was published in the 2005 *Mays Literary Anthology*.

Alex Wylie
'The Star and the Ditch', 'Judas' and 'Four Versions of Borges' have previously been published in *PN Review*; 'Ekphrasis' and 'Kensho River' have appeared in *Stand*.